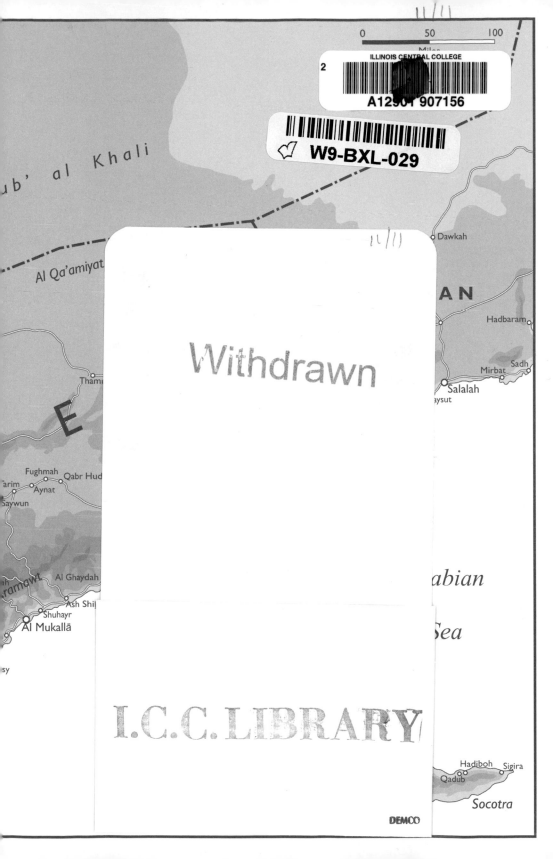

HIGH-VALUE
TARGET

ADST-DACOR DIPLOMATS AND DIPLOMACY SERIES

Series Editor: Margery Boichel Thompson

Since 1776, extraordinary men and women have represented the United States abroad under all sorts of circumstances. What they did and how and why they did it remain little known to their compatriots. In 1995 the Association for Diplomatic Studies and Training (ADST) and DACOR, an organization of foreign affairs professionals, created the Diplomats and Diplomacy book series to increase public knowledge and appreciation of the role of American diplomats in world history. The series seeks to demystify diplomacy through the stories of those who have conducted U.S. foreign relations, as they lived, influenced, and reported them. Edmund J. Hull's *High-Value Target*, forty-fourth in the series, provides a timely example and useful lessons.

OTHER TITLES IN THE SERIES

HERMAN J. COHEN, *Intervening in Africa: Superpower Peacemaking in a Troubled Continent*

CHARLES T. CROSS, *Born a Foreigner: A Memoir of the American Presence in Asia*

BRANDON GROVE, *Behind Embassy Walls: The Life and Times of an American Diplomat*

PARKER T. HART, *Saudi Arabia and the United States: Birth of a Security Partnership*

CAMERON R. HUME, *Mission to Algiers: Diplomacy by Engagement*

DENNIS KUX, *The United States and Pakistan, 1947–2000: Disenchanted Allies*

JANE C. LOEFFLER, *The Architecture of Diplomacy: Building America's Embassies*

TERRY MCNAMARA, *Escape with Honor: My Last Hours in Vietnam*

WILLIAM B. MILAM, *Bangladesh and Pakistan: Flirting with Failure in Muslim South Asia*

ROBERT H. MILLER, *Vietnam and Beyond: A Diplomat's Cold War Education*

DAVID D. NEWSOM, *Witness to a Changing World*

RONALD E. NEUMANN, *The Other War: Winning and Losing in Afghanistan*

RICHARD B. PARKER, ed., *The October War: A Retrospective*

YALE RICHMOND, *Practicing Public Diplomacy: A Cold War Odyssey*

HOWARD B. SCHAFFER, *The Limits of Influence: America's Role in Kashmir*

HOWARD R. SIMPSON, *Bush Hat, Black Tie: Adventures of a Foreign Service Officer*

ULRICH STRAUS, *The Anguish of Surrender: Japanese POWs of World War II*

JAMES STEPHENSON, *Losing the Golden Hour: An Insider's View of Iraq's Reconstruction*

HIGH-VALUE TARGET

COUNTERING AL QAEDA IN YEMEN

AMB. EDMUND J. HULL (RET.)

FOREWORD BY AMB. MARC GROSSMAN

An ADST-DACOR Diplomats and Diplomacy Book

Potomac Books
Washington, D.C.

Library of Congress Cataloging-in-Publication Data
Hull, Edmund J. (Edmund James), 1949–
High-value target : countering al Qaeda in Yemen / Edmund J. Hull ; foreword by Marc Grossman. — 1st ed.
p. cm. — (ADST-DACOR diplomats and diplomacy series)
Includes bibliographical references and index.
ISBN 978-1-59797-679-4 (hardcover : alk. paper)
1. Terrorism—Yemen—History—20th century. 2. Terrorism—Prevention. 3. Yemen—Politics and government. 4. Qaida (Organization)—History. 5. Yemen—Foreign relations—21st century. 6. Yemen—Foreign relations—United States. I. Title.
HV6433.Y4H85 2011
363.32509533—dc22

                                                                              2011004712

To my wife, Amal, who shared the risks and the rewards,
and to the American and Yemeni staff of Embassy Sanaa,
whose will found ways.

CONTENTS

Yemeni Cast of Characters

YEMENI OFFICIALS

Ali Abdullah Saleh, president of the Republic of Yemen

Abdulkarim al-Iryani, presidential adviser

Abu Bakr al-Qirby, minister of foreign affairs

Rashad al-Alimi, interior minister

Col. Yahya Saleh, commander of the Central Security Forces (nephew of the president)

Abdulwahab al-Hajri, Yemeni ambassador in Washington

AL QAEDA

Qaed Salim Sinan (Abu Ali al-Harithi), leader of al Qaeda in Yemen

Mohamed Hamdi al-Ahdal (Abu Assem al-Mekki), al Qaeda financier and
subordinate leader in Yemen

Abd al-Rahim al-Nashiri, chief of al Qaeda operations in the Arabian Peninsula

Jamal al-Badawi, co-conspirator in attack on the USS *Cole*

Jaber A. Elbaneh, American Yemeni on FBI's Most Wanted Terrorists list

Fawaz al-Rabi'a, de facto leader of al Qaeda in Yemen following Abu Ali's death

Nasir al-Wahayshi, leader of revived al Qaeda in Yemen and later Arabian Peninsula

ABBREVIATIONS

AQAP	Al Qaeda in the Arabian Peninsula
CENTCOM	Central Command
CIA	Central Intelligence Agency
CSF	Central Security Forces
CSG	Counterterrorism Security Group
DoD	Department of Defense
EAC	Emergency Action Committee
EU	European Union
FBI	Federal Bureau of Investigation
FY	fiscal year
GCC	Gulf Cooperation Council
HVT	High-value target
IMF	International Monetary Fund
JCS	Joint Chiefs of Staff
MEPI	Middle East Partnership Initiative
NCIS	Naval Criminal Investigation Service
NDI	National Democratic Institute
NEA	Bureau of Near Eastern Affairs
NSA	National Security Agency
NSC	National Security Council
PISCES	Personal Identification Secure Comparison and Evaluation System
PSO	Political Security Organization

S/CT	The Secretary of State's Counterterrorism Office
SCER	Supreme Committee for Elections and Referenda
TIP	Terrorist Interdiction Program
UN	United Nations
UNDP	United Nations Development Program
USAID	United States Agency for International Development
USDA	United States Department of Agriculture
USIA	United States Information Agency
WAE	When Actually Employed (status of State Department retirees brought back to duty)
YSOF	Yemeni Special Operation Forces

FOREWORD

Amb. Edmund Hull has written a timely and important book that describes how active, comprehensive, and modern American diplomacy protects and promotes U.S. interests at home and abroad. Ambassador Hull's description of his years as U.S. ambassador to Yemen will appeal to experts who study that difficult and fascinating country, to citizens committed to understanding what it will take to defeat violent extremism, to students of diplomacy, and, crucially, to those who hope to pursue a career in diplomacy.

This book is a reminder that, even though years have passed since September 11, 2001, the effects of the attacks in New York, Washington, and Pennsylvania are still profound. Ambassador Hull's description of being in the Pentagon on that fateful day is compelling and helps younger readers understand the attack's impact on the United States, especially on senior government officials. He brings home 9/11's continuing influence: the attempted bombing of Northwest Airlines flight 253 on December 25, 2009, was allegedly carried out by a terrorist born in Nigeria but trained in Yemen. He also rightly highlights former secretary of state Colin Powell's admonition that the defeat of terrorism cannot be accomplished by a fearful America or an America "hunkered down," afraid to engage in the world.

The ambassador writes of his first meeting with Yemeni president Ali Abdullah Saleh as being focused on terrorism; he wanted Saleh to know that al Qaeda in Yemen had "names and faces." His early encounters with his embassy staff are at Emergency Action Committee meetings, trying to balance the need to protect American lives and influence Yemeni society. Ambassador Hull also dealt with the aftermath of the al

Qaeda attack on the USS *Cole* and supported U.S. law enforcement as it tracked down the murderers and encouraged the Yemeni government to cooperate.

This is also a book about how modern diplomacy is carried out. Hull's reference to earlier ambassadors in Sanaa reminds us that most progress in diplomacy is not linear and that diplomats take the baton from a predecessor, run the race as quickly and as effectively as possible, and then hand that baton off to a successor. Hull also recognizes that twenty-first-century diplomacy, especially in a nation where al Qaeda is present, requires a comprehensive strategy that draws on what is today described as "the whole of government" approach. He knows that for the United States to be successful, the Yemeni population has to turn against al Qaeda and that "we would have to use the entire tool kit: diplomacy to create political will, intelligence to locate targets and defend ourselves, security or military forces to capture or kill the operatives, economic assistance, and public diplomacy to win popular support." He explains this to Yemeni leaders as "no development without security; no security without development."

The ambassador mobilizes the talents and resources available to him on his Country Team: the United States Agency for International Development, public diplomacy, law enforcement, the Central Command, the Joint Chiefs of Staff, visiting senior officials from Washington, including the vice president, and even, at one point, the U.S. Coast Guard. Using a broader definition of human security and combining it with a whole-of-government approach is the foundation for what Philip Bobbitt has called a strategy of preclusion, in which extremism is defeated not only militarily (although this will sometimes remain necessary), but also by a larger, comprehensive strategy of diplomacy supported by development.

This book is also testament to the proposition that the type of people we choose to be diplomats and the resources we give them matters. While most of Hull's book takes place in Yemen, his trips back to Washington to seek the right staff and the right resources to carry out American policy are crucial parts of this story. The importance he puts on recruiting people with language skills, with the curiosity and the desire to understand a country such as Yemen, and with the courage to serve on the front lines of the battle against extremism are reminders that the quality of diplomacy is very much affected by the people who do it. There is one other point to focus on here: the personal debt Hull expresses to his wife, Amal. The reader can feel his loss in having to go to Yemen first without her and the important role she then plays as a representative in her own right in connecting with Yemen's art, culture, and history.

If the diplomacy described in this book was so effective, why were the passengers on Northwest Airlines flight 253 almost victims of terrorism in December 2009? Part of the answer lies in the truth that progress is not linear; long-term success comes only from persistent attention. Yemenis got distracted by tribal conflict and paid the price of the jailbreaks illustrated by Hull in the book. Washington may have put Yemen in the "done" category and moved on to the next set of equally important and difficult challenges. Whatever the causes, this book demonstrates that the struggle against extremism will not only be comprehensive but also long.

I first met Edmund Hull in the summer of 1979 when we were both staff assistants to then Assistant Secretary of State for Near Eastern and South Asian Affairs Harold H. Saunders. Hull had returned to Washington from Jerusalem; I had just returned from a first tour in Pakistan. We could never have foreseen what was headed in our direction: the taking of American hostages in Iran, the burning of the U.S. embassy in Islamabad, the destruction of the U.S. embassy in Tripoli, attacks on Americans throughout the Middle East and elsewhere. Edmund and I tried to help our leaders grapple with crisis after crisis. We forged a bond that has lasted to this day. We also, I believe, adopted an outlook on the need to defeat violent extremism because we lived it so closely, so early in our careers.

Neither the first to be told nor surely the last, this story is of an American diplomat's attempts to turn a country and its leaders from being a "target" of Washington to being a "partner" of the United States. It suggests what much of American diplomacy is going to be like for the coming decades and deserves close attention.

Amb. Marc Grossman
Arlington, Virginia
January 2011

PREFACE

"The U.S. government must identify and prioritize actual or potential terrorist sanctuaries. For each, it should have a realistic strategy to keep possible terrorists insecure and on the run, using all elements of national power. We should reach out, listen to, and work with other countries that can help."

—*The 9/11 Commission Report*

"In Yemen, we are working to avert the possibility of another Afghanistan."

—*President George W. Bush, March 11, 2002,*
Remarks on the Six-Month Anniversary of the September 11th Attacks

On September 11, 2001, I was meeting in the Pentagon when the third hijacked airplane impacted nearby. I had a good idea of the enemy that had struck the American homeland after having recently culminated two years as deputy, then acting coordinator for counterterrorism in the Department of State. That day I was in the Pentagon, however, as ambassador-designate to Yemen, and within the month, I had arrived in Yemen, an al Qaeda stronghold, with a presidential mandate to keep it from becoming another Afghanistan. The three years that followed, in which al Qaeda's leadership was decapitated and its ranks depleted in Yemen, are the subject of this book.

Our challenge was to develop and implement a strategy to deny al Qaeda a safe haven in Yemen. We had no models, so we created one. With precious few resources, nothing close to what would be expended in Afghanistan or Iraq, we improvised. We used funds from the sale of surplus U.S. agriculture products to finance development in remote tribal areas, built training facilities from discarded tires, and created a Yemeni Coast Guard from cast-off boats. This is a story of making do. And it is a story of a small group of Americans—diplomats and military personnel, intelligence and development experts—partnering with Yemeni officials. No small part of our achievement was the slow and uneven progress in creating within Yemen's leadership the will, and within Yemen's security forces the capacity, to take the lead in a broad counterterrorism effort.

We took a broad view of counterterrorism far beyond the narrow cooperation of intelligence agencies or military forces, which is the usual focus of counterterrorism literature. For us, equipping a hospital in Ma'rib, conducting free and fair parliamentary elections, and empowering the women of Yemen were important objectives in the struggle against extremism. For each, we found partners and programs that allowed us to contribute and to register gains.

In a sense, our greatest impediment was not the insecurity in which we worked or the paucity of resources, but rather the mutual suspicions that corroded the partnership we were attempting to build. In both Washington and Sanaa, the debate was cast in terms of "Yemen: partner or target?" It was essentially a diplomatic question: how could we make Yemeni leaders, people, and tribes a partner in the war against al Qaeda, and not fight our true enemy in a way that swelled his ranks or elicited protection from them?

In Sanaa we were fortunate to have the shrewdness of President Ali Abdullah Saleh, the wisdom of his adviser Abdulkarim al-Iryani, the dedication of Interior Minister Rashad al-Alimi, and the competence of Social Fund director Abdulkarim al-Arhabi. In Washington, I worked for a "dream team" in the Department of State: Secretary Colin Powell, Deputy Secretary Richard Armitage, Under Secretary Marc Grossman, Assistant Secretary Bill Burns, and Deputy Assistant Secretary Ryan Crocker. CIA director George Tenet and FBI director Bob Mueller provided constant attention and support. While we were far from his primary concern, President George W. Bush's personal engagement with President Saleh laid the foundation of our venture.

Embassy Sanaa's country team, its American and Yemeni staff, and the temporary duty personnel, who often outnumbered the permanently assigned, are the heroes of my tale. Too numerous and, in many cases, too sensitive to mention by name, they found ways of producing results when risk far outweighed resources. The success we

INTRODUCTION

"Where al Qaeda and its allies attempt to establish a foothold—whether in Somalia or Yemen or elsewhere—they must be confronted by growing pressure and strong partnerships."

—*Barack Obama, December 1, 2009*

Denying safe havens to al Qaeda has been a consistent theme of both the George W. Bush and the Barack Obama administrations as has an ongoing, if sometimes faltering, effort to do so particularly in Yemen. Why are safe havens deemed so critical? Why is Yemen so problematic? Brief answers to these questions usefully frame the account of counterterrorism in Yemen (2001–4) that follows.

COUNTERTERRORISM: SIMPLY CONCEIVED

In the winter of 2008–9, some 250 individuals gathered at Fort McNair in Washington, D.C., to undertake for Gen. David Petraeus a strategic assessment for the Central Command of which he had recently become the commander. The assessment was broken down into both geographic and functional teams. I was asked to head the counterterrorism team, which included a range of experts from USAID to special operations. Over the next four months, we interacted with many other intelligence experts, academics, and practitioners. This experience crystallized for us the essence of the problem and a general strategy to confront it. In a sense, it was an opportunity to conceptualize what we, and many others, had been doing as practical matters to counter terrorism.

Successful counterterrorism begins, in my experience, with a clear definition of who the enemy is. A great failing in the "Global War on Terror," as conceived and executed under the Bush administration, was a conflation of threats. Presidential speeches throughout the period were replete with references to "the enemy" not further defined.[1] The most dramatic consequence of this conflation was the spurious linkage of Iraq and al Qaeda, which served as a primary justification for the invasion of Iraq. The professionals knew better.[2] In stark contrast, the annual assessments of the director of central intelligence (then) and the director of national intelligence (now) are models of clarity. They lucidly state and prioritize the groups that threaten the United States. Since 9/11 at the top of this list has been al Qaeda, namely because of its unrelenting intent and global capability to attack the United States.

Al Qaeda itself comprises al Qaeda central, under the leadership of Osama bin Laden and Ayman al-Zawahiri, believed to be located in western Pakistan; al Qaeda franchises, including al Qaeda in Iraq and Al Qaeda in the Arabian Peninsula (AQAP); and al Qaeda cells throughout the world. The threat is complicated both by al Qaeda allies—the Taliban in Afghanistan, Lashkar-e-Tayyiba in Pakistan, and others—and by homegrown terrorist cells in places such as London. Such connections are interesting and important. Accounting for these complexities reflects reality; speaking of "the enemy," so as to lump together al Qaeda, Hamas, Hezbollah, or even hostile regimes such as Iran, only leads to confusion.[3] "Name the enemy" is a good rule of thumb. Both in this introduction and the chapters that follow, the enemy is al Qaeda.

How does one think about the intricate phenomenon of global al Qaeda terrorism? In our work for CENTCOM, we found a simple medical analogy to provide a useful concept.[4] There are political, social, and economic conditions that create the environment in which al Qaeda is likely to prosper. Chief among these conditions, I have found, are foreign occupation, corruption, and lack of economic opportunity.[5] In the case of al Qaeda, an extremist ideology is conceived as a response by Osama bin Laden and Ayman al-Zawahiri.[6] This ideology motivates individuals who act like viruses to respond violently to the offending conditions.[7] These viruses not only contaminate the original host country, but also spread throughout the international system, infecting other countries and other regions where conditions are propitious.

Historically, al Qaeda and other terrorist groups have needed safe havens in which to incubate their virus. They have needed physical space in which to organize, train, plan, and equip for operations. (How many of these functions are being done or might be done virtually is yet to be seen, but al Qaeda uses the Internet effec-

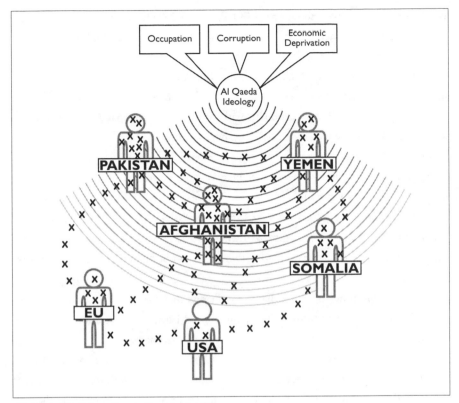

Al Qaeda Terrorism: Simply Conceived

tively.) Grant al Qaeda expansive safe haven—as in Afghanistan prior to 9/11—and al Qaeda's capability waxes. Deny al Qaeda safe haven—as in Yemen 2001–4—and its capability wanes. A primary objective of our counterterrorism efforts should be to deny, or, at a minimum, challenge, any of al Qaeda's safe havens so that it is unable to sustain attacks against the U.S. homeland that would fundamentally alter Americans' way of life.[8]

Safe havens should be conceived as relative. The 9/11 plot was hatched not only in Afghanistan, but also in many other countries, most notably Germany. The al Qaeda virus exists in various degrees in many places around the world. Counterterrorism efforts must be global because the network is global. However, clearly some places are safer than others for al Qaeda. Again as part of the CENTCOM exercise, we informally asked experts to rate locations as safe havens on a scale of one to ten, with one being the United States and ten being Afghanistan pre-9/11 under the Taliban. So conceived, experts tended to rate parts of Pakistan and Afghanistan in the seven–eight range and parts of Yemen in the four–five range. These ratings reflect both the size of al Qaeda's presence and the degree of impunity it enjoys.

In the extreme case of Afghanistan, Presidents Bush and Obama have opted for direct U.S. military involvement, using a counterinsurgency model as was used in Iraq. There are generally two problems with applying this approach. First, it is enormously expensive. Second, it can be easily portrayed by al Qaeda as U.S. occupation and thus can generate great numbers of new *mujahideen*, or "holy warriors." In most cases, direct U.S. military operational involvement tends to be counterproductive because U.S. forces themselves have the effect of a "virus" that triggers indigenous "antibodies" acting in concert with al Qaeda as in Afghanistan and Iraq.[9] Generally, a superior strategy is an indirect approach whereby the United States trains and equips indigenous counterterrorism forces that then act as antibodies to protect the host from the al Qaeda virus.

At the same time, the underlying conditions that facilitate al Qaeda's radicalization should also be addressed. While the second Bush administration badly overreached in trying to re-create the Middle East in its own democratic image, the more modest reform objectives of the Middle East Partnership Initiative (MEPI) of the administration's first term were apt complements to its counterterrorism efforts. If the United States does not assist the concerned governments with addressing the root causes, then it risks winning tactical victories against al Qaeda but losing the war. A strategy that relies primarily on intelligence and strikes brings with it the frustrations of the classic "whack-a-mole" game.

To sum up, an effective strategy to deny al Qaeda safe haven in Yemen requires that the Yemeni government and people reject al Qaeda (the threatening virus) and develop the indigenous capability (the antibodies) to counter this threat while addressing the fundamental conditions and ideology that allow al Qaeda to generate a limitless supply of mujahideen.

POPULOUS, POOR, AND PREOCCUPIED

In Yemen, a population of some 22 million people—half of whom are under the age of fifteen—is widely dispersed over a territory the size of California and Pennsylvania combined.[10] Low-lying coasts give way to mountains in the interior as one moves east from the Red Sea and north from the Gulf of Aden. Many of the mountains are painstakingly terraced, which evidences centuries of cultivation, and most villages are perched on summits or ridgelines for security. In the far northeast, Yemen becomes desert and merges with Saudi Arabia's "empty quarter," or Al Rub' al Khali. Yemen is a spectacularly beautiful place, one that has spawned a rugged and independent population.

Unlike most countries of the Arabian Peninsula, Yemen has only modest amounts of oil and gas, although these nevertheless constitute the majority of exports and fund the public budget.[11] Per capita income is only about $950 per year; about 40 percent of the population is poor. Yemen was famous for its coffee; the port of Mocha on the Red Sea gave its name to a blend still featured in your local Starbucks—Arabian Mocha Sanani. However, for centuries, Yemenis have indulged in their favorite pastime of chewing leaves from the *khat* shrub, which contain a natural, amphetamine-like stimulant. A profitable cash crop, khat has steadily displaced not only coffee, but also fruits and vegetables in Yemen's countryside. About a quarter of Yemen's water consumption and 11 percent of its agricultural land is used in khat cultivation.[12]

GOVERNANCE A CHALLENGE

Yemen is one of the few parts of the Arab world that has retained a large measure of independence throughout its history. True, the British controlled the strategic port of Aden and its hinterland from 1832 to 1967. Also, the Ottomans repeatedly tried to rule the north (from 1517 to 1635 and from 1872 to 1918), but their control was limited to the coast and a few major cities. By contrast, indigenous authority in parts of Yemen has been long-standing. Religious authority became prominent in Yemen with the arrival of Imam Yahya al-Hadi ila'l Haqq in 897, and the Zaidi dynasty thus established continued until the second half of the twentieth century. With the departure of the Ottomans in 1918, the Zaidi Imam Yahya ruled independently as did his successors until 1962 when Yemeni army officers seized power and created a republic. The resulting civil war brought in the Egyptians on the side of the republicans and the Saudis on the side of the imam's supporters. As had others before, Egypt found its intervention in Yemen costly and unproductive, and withdrew its forces in 1967. Saudi Arabia formally recognized the republic in 1970 but continued to meddle in Yemeni tribal politics to weaken the Yemeni regime. Meanwhile, with the dissolution of its empire, the British retreated from Aden in 1967 under pressure from Yemeni national liberation movements, which established a Marxist regime.

The Yemeni republic in the north was plagued by a series of coups until the arrival of Col. Ali Abdullah Saleh in 1978. Against all odds, Saleh consolidated power in North Yemen and brought stability. He subsequently engineered a union with South Yemen in 1990 after its Marxist regime became an orphan of *perestroika* with the Soviet Union's collapse. With encouragement from Saudi Arabia, some southerners attempted to reverse that union in 1994, but Saleh quickly defeated the rebellion with significant help from the northern tribes and the mujahideen who had returned from Afghanistan in the wake of the Soviet withdrawal. Saleh reconciled with the Saudis with the Treaty of Jeddah in 2000, which also resolved a long-disputed border. Thereafter, the Saudis gradually reduced their direct involvement with Yemeni tribes and increased support for Saleh's government. Clearly, the dominant force in Yemeni politics for the past quarter century has been Ali Abdullah Saleh. While cunning has been his dominant personal trait, his historic accomplishments—consolidating his rule, unifying North and South Yemen, and reconciling with Saudi Arabia—evidence a formidable strategic vision. Expanding that vision to address the al Qaeda threat has proven to be the central and continuing challenge to counterterrorism in Yemen.

Where does President Saleh's and his government's writ run? The Yemeni military and security forces can project themselves throughout the country on an ad hoc basis, but to operate effectively in many places they require the support or acquiescence of the tribes. The notion that the central government controls the capital and perhaps major cities and that all else is chaos is a persistent myth.[13] The problem is that significant areas—Ma'rib, Al Jawf, Shabwah, and Sa'dah in the north, and Abyan in the south—are deprived of government resources and attention. As a result, the tribes there feel only a tenuous connection with the central government. Health facilities and schools are unequipped, unstaffed, and often dilapidated. The president himself makes an occasional tour, which causes a burst of effort, but ministers rarely visit. The tribes grow restive, and frequently younger, more aggressive members take foreigners hostage to compel government attention. Too often these situations are resolved through concessions by the government, which only encourage further hostage-taking. The resulting insecurity adversely impacts development as foreign aid workers are pulled back and projects abandoned. This vicious circle of no security and no development provides al Qaeda space in which to operate.

Yemen's governance problem extends beyond the deprived areas, however. Yemen has a multiparty system. The former communist regime of South Yemen has evolved into the Yemeni Socialist Party supported by a small fraction of the population. More formidable is the Islamic-based party Islah (Reform), which has broad appeal. As in Turkey, Islah politicians in Yemen capitalize on the inevitable corruption that characterizes a regime that has retained power for more than a quarter of a century. A kind of sclerosis afflicts Yemen's body politic. Budgets are opaque. Many government services are funded but not performed. Foreign donors are daunted. In 2009 Transparency International ranked Yemen 154 out of 180 countries in its corruption perception index.[14]

TRIBES

In Yemen, tribes are a significant factor in both governance and counterterrorism. In the south, tribal affiliations have been attenuated by decades of Marxist rule, but in the north, tribal and clan identity are generally stronger than national identity. The phenomenon is evident even in the capital of Sanaa, where government sway is most pronounced. Tribal chiefs regularly travel under the protection of their own bodyguards, and the interior minister's efforts to restrict weapons in the capital are well intentioned but often ineffective. A visit to a paramount sheikh, such as the late Abdullah al-Ahmar, in his Sanaa residence is not unlike a visit to the American embassy with its independent security force and extraterritoriality. Travel in the tribal regions, specifically Ma'rib, Al Jawf, and Shabwah, is coordinated through the government, which provides a security escort, but also with the tribes' sheikhs who might provide an escort, too, through their territories.

The tribes of the north are well armed. Young men acquire Kalashnikovs in their early teens, and their weapons are never far from their sides, even when they are eating or drinking tea. Heavier weapons are also plentiful. Vast caches of weapons purchased by the central government from the tribes include rocket-propelled grenades, artillery, and surface-to-air missiles. When the central government undertakes the use of force in tribal areas without consent, tribal resistance can be formidable.

The Yemeni tribes in general, however, have no affinity for al Qaeda and its ideology. Connections that exist tend to be familial, not tribal. An uncle with al Qaeda connections might well pass those associations on to nephews. Yemeni politics do not necessarily break down along tribal lines. Both Ali Abdullah Saleh and the al-Ahmars, who have led the opposition Islah party, come from the Hashid tribal federation.

Yemen's tribal leaders are also subject to the slow but inexorable effects of centralization and modernization. The prominent sheikhs retain strongholds not only in their tribal areas but also in Sanaa, which mean they live increasingly under significant government influence. This trend is encouraged by the subtle but effective influence of wives who prefer the relative comfort of the city to life in the tribal regions.

Saleh's rapprochement with the Saudis also significantly enhanced central government control. Previously, Saudi largesse to individual tribal sheikhs was intended to undermine central authority in the tribal regions. The frequent visits of tribal sheikhs to Riyadh showed the importance of this connection. In the wake of the Treaty of Jeddah, the Saudis have generally restricted their support to grandfathering pre-existing arrangements.

Yemeni tribes serve the additional function of providing their young men with an identity and a social support system. While often poor and therefore susceptible to offers of employment in the diaspora as policemen in the United Arab Emirates or mujahideen in Afghanistan, Yemeni youth generally are not alienated or deracinated.

ISLAM: STRONG AND MODERATE

Yemenis are a religious people. Islam arrived in 630 soon after the revelation of the Koran to the Prophet Mohamed. The Shia Zaidi sect predominates in the north and northwest, while the Shafi'i school of Sunni Islam predominates in the south and southeast. Historically, unlike in Iraq or Pakistan, there has been little sectarian conflict between the two.[15] Yemen has no indigenous equivalent to the extremist Wahhabi school of Islam that dominates in Saudi Arabia, although Yemeni leaders are mindful and concerned about the spread of Wahhabi thought by way of Saudi funding of mosques. Similarly, there is no traditional system of schools (*madrasas*) producing Pakistani-style Taliban. Nevertheless, Yemen is not exempt from the regional trend toward greater religious conservatism as indicated by the increasing adoption of Gulf-style veiling (*hijab*).

THE AL QAEDA CONNECTION:
LONG-STANDING AND PERSISTENT

Yemen has figured as the location for some of al Qaeda's earliest and most successful operations. In 1992 al Qaeda operatives struck at U.S. military forces in Aden as they were deploying to Somalia. Later, in 1998, Yemen served as a staging ground for the successful al Qaeda attacks on the U.S. embassies in Nairobi and Dar es Salaam. In 2000 al Qaeda operatives successfully attacked in Aden and nearly sank the USS *Cole*. In the 2001–4 period (the subject of the account that follows), al Qaeda carried out numerous but significantly declining attacks against Yemeni targets and plotted against American ones as well. But, after a respite of several years, al Qaeda terrorism reappeared after 2006 to include a suicide attack against the American embassy in Sanaa, the 2009 attempt to destroy Northwest Airlines flight 253 on approach to Detroit on Christmas Day, and the 2010 plot to conceal bombs aboard FedEx and UPS flights to the United States.

A significant factor in al Qaeda's persistent presence in Yemen has been the opportunity that jihads afford Yemeni youth. Yemen provided many of the mujahideen in the U.S.-backed campaign that ultimately forced the Soviets out of Afghanistan. Upon their return to Yemen, they retained their connections with the developing al Qaeda movement. Unsurprisingly, Yemenis have always therefore constituted a disproportionate number of prisoners at the Guantánamo Bay detention facility.[16] Given the centrality of family and clan in Yemen, it is not surprising either that these mujahideen connections to al Qaeda frequently expand to include brothers, cousins, nephews, uncles, et al. This long-standing social geography makes Yemen fertile ground for al Qaeda recruitment.

A leading theorist of the jihadist movement, Abu Bakr Naji, has cited five factors conducive to jihadist safe havens, or areas he terms "regions of savagery":

- The presence of geographic depth and topography (that) permits . . . the establishment of regions . . . of savagery
- The weakness of the ruling regime and the weakness of the centralization of its power in the peripheries . . . and sometimes in internal regions . . .
- The presence of jihadist, Islamic expansion being propagated in these regions
- The nature of the people in these regions . . .
- The distribution of weapons among people who are in those regions [17]

Yemen features high on Al Naji's list of potential safe havens, while Egypt, Iraq, Syria, and other historic centers of Islam do not. In this thinking, Yemen is not bounded by the "borders [of] the United Nations," meaning those internationally recognized, but rather merges with Saudi Arabia to the north and Oman to the east. Nor does Al Naji expect al Qaeda to control the entire region, as he observes that "the region of savagery is usually a city, or a village, or two cities, or a district, or part of a large city."[18]

Objective conditions and jihadist strategy destine Yemen to be a significant theater in the struggle against al Qaeda. Jihadist thinkers have thought through their strategies for winning there. Those who would deny al Qaeda safe haven in Yemen need to reflect on their strategies as well.

CHAPTER ONE

AL QAEDA STRIKES A BLOW

T he Pentagon had enhanced its security. Or so it seemed as I processed
through the South Parking entrance on my way to see Vice Adm. Timo-
thy J. Keating. He had been named commander of the Fifth Fleet, which
patrolled the Persian Gulf and, until the USS *Cole* attack on October 12, 2000, refu-
eled at Aden Port in Yemen. I had been nominated by President George W. Bush and
confirmed by the Senate as ambassador to Yemen, and I was making the most of my
last month in Washington by networking in order to go to Yemen's capital, Sanaa, and
represent not only State, but also the National Security Council (NSC), Department
of Defense (DoD), Joint Chiefs of Staff (JCS), Central Intelligence Agency (CIA),
and Federal Bureau of Investigation (FBI). Since October 2000, counterterrorism had
been the central issue in our relations with Yemen. I knew from representing State on
Richard A. Clarke's Counterterrorism Security Group (CSG) over the last two years
that counterterrorism was inherently an interagency issue. Success depended on the
various parts of the U.S. government working as a whole. As the chief of mission, I
would have the president's mandate to supervise and primary responsibility for all U.S.
counterterrorism activities in Yemen. Later that day, I was scheduled to visit the FBI's
counterterrorism office to receive an update on the *Cole* case, but first I looked forward
to hearing Admiral Keating's perspective.

While the security guard verified my ID and scanned my briefcase, first reports
buzzed through the security post of a bizarre incident in which a plane had crashed
into the World Trade Center. A light aircraft, I assumed, and limited damage. Was
it an accident or something sinister? When news of a second crash followed, I knew

my counterterrorism colleagues in Washington would be heading for the secure video teleconferencing facilities in the White House and other situation rooms.

A similar incident only a few months earlier would have been my responsibility at State. My predecessor, Mike Sheehan, had taken over S/CT, the counterterrorism office that reports directly to the secretary of state, in 1998. We had worked together previously on UN affairs when I had been responsible for peacekeeping operations. A brilliant and abrasive nonbureaucrat, Mike had a mandate from Secretary of State Madeleine Albright to ramp up counterterrorism diplomacy in the wake of the vehicle bombings at our embassies in Nairobi and Dar es Salaam on August 7, 1998. He had worked before that for Dick Clarke. Ever the consummate bureaucratic entrepreneur, Dick had championed Mike's appointment to shake up State's counterterrorism operations. With the end of the Clinton administration imminent, Mike had moved on to help Kofi Annan with UN peacekeeping.

Named acting director of S/CT after Mike's departure, I had been assigned my first task from Secretary of State–designate Colin Powell to organize a transition briefing on counterterrorism. It was mid-December 2000, and I was impressed that Powell was making terrorism one of his top priorities. My first call was to Clarke.

"Dick, the Secretary wants to hear about counterterrorism, and it would be best if he also sees the CSG in action," I proposed. Dick needed no convincing. Our agenda to focus the new administration on the al Qaeda threat was a collective priority. So, on December 20, we gathered Cofer Black, director of the CIA's Counterterrorism Center; Dale Watson, assistant director for the FBI's Counterterrorism Division; Brian Sheridan, assistant secretary of defense for special operations/low-intensity conflict; and JCS and other representatives. Powell, who later cited the briefing in his testimony to the 9/11 Commission, was attentive. We centered the issue squarely on al Qaeda and its safe haven in Afghanistan.[1]

When Cofer Black predicted flatly that al Qaeda would attack the United States, the secretary challenged, "What algorithm supports that?"

"Thirty years of experience, Mr. Secretary," Cofer replied.

Brian Sheridan, later cited by the 9/11 Commission for having tried to bring the Office of the Secretary of Defense to a more robust military effort against al Qaeda, pled to keep the CSG functioning although he himself would be leaving the administration. "Never," he said, "in my entire career have I seen a better interagency process."

For my part, I noted our continuing diplomatic efforts to enforce the hard-won UN arms embargo against the Taliban embodied in UN Security Council resolution

1333 and urged the secretary to give priority to recruiting Mike Sheehan's permanent successor. (I was later pleased that Powell did so by naming Air Force brigadier general Frank Taylor, which allowed me to hand over the reins in July and concentrate on my appointment to Yemen.) I also noted that Congress had established S/CT as an office directly reporting to the secretary. Previous administrations, including Albright's, had attempted to downgrade S/CT by subordinating it to lesser officials.

Powell's parting remark was typically astute: "The administration will confront terrorism, but we will not hunker down in bunkers and allow ourselves to be terrorized."

We later learned that Powell had told his deputy, Rich Armitage, to obtain a similar terrorism briefing and to follow the issue closely. He did so. In the Bush administration, we would have ready access not only to Under Secretary of Political Affairs Marc Grossman, but the deputy secretary and the secretary as well. By contrast, in the Clinton administration, the only seventh floor principal to whom S/CT had regular access was the Under Secretary for Political Affairs Tom Pickering, a masterful diplomat. Secretary Albright had taken her daily briefing from the head of Diplomatic Security, whose mission was to protect diplomats, not to pursue al Qaeda.

The transition had gone well. Later, the CSG repeated its al Qaeda briefing for the president's national security adviser, Condoleezza Rice, who decided to keep Dick Clarke and his team on. Brian Sheridan never had a chance to brief Donald Rumsfeld, whose building I was entering on September 11.

Admiral Keating was cordial. We briefly noted the events of New York but then proceeded to discuss future collaboration in Yemen. As I had done previously at my Senate confirmation hearing, I stressed my commitment to successfully completing the investigation of the *Cole* attack and bringing its perpetrators to justice. I had already made an effort in this regard during my visit to Aden and Sanaa the previous March. Gaining Yemeni cooperation was like pulling teeth, and I was to be the "dentist in residence." I wanted the U.S. Navy to have no doubt that the case would have my personal attention.

At the same time, it bothered me that the navy had no plans to return to Aden. Based on what I knew from my previous work, al Qaeda kept score differently than we did. The U.S. government likes metrics—numbers of terrorist incidents, casualties, and so forth. My office S/CT annually published these statistics in *Patterns of Global Terrorism*.[2] I had been responsible for the publication in April 2001. *Patterns of Global Terrorism* was a useful tool because it gathered together in unclassified form reliable information about the bewildering array of international terrorist groups and their state sponsors. It also emphasized our formal designations of "foreign terrorist organizations" and "state sponsors of terrorism." Both congressionally mandated lists had significant political impact. State sponsors—particularly Libya and North Korea at that time—chafed at this designation. But the number crunching, per se, was not especially helpful. Major terrorist events, such as the bombing of our East Africa embassies, and minor ones, including attacks on Colombian pipelines, were counted equally for statistical purposes.

Instead, al Qaeda aimed to transcend divisions in the Islamic world by reestablishing a fundamentalist caliphate akin to the regimes that had ruled following the creation of Islam in the seventh century. Its immediate objectives were to undermine moderate Islamic regimes and to force the United States to either withdraw its forces from the Islamic world or bleed them as long as they stayed. Hence, al Qaeda recorded as major successes the U.S. withdrawal from Lebanon in 1984 (a result of Hezbollah, not al Qaeda, activity) and the similar withdrawal from Somalia in 1994 after the "Black Hawk Down" incident.[3] I was concerned that the U.S. Navy now appeared to consider Aden Port a "no-go" zone. True, Djibouti across the Gulf of Aden in Africa supplied our practical needs. However, the political problem remained: al Qaeda's success in attacking the *Cole* would not be completely reversed until the navy returned to a secure Aden. My view: the navy should go securely wherever it needed.[4]

As we reviewed the situation and our upcoming responsibilities, our meeting room was jolted. What force could shake a building the size of the Pentagon? The answer came quickly from the admiral's staff: a commercial airliner had slammed into the adjoining sector a short walk from our room. Smoke was already filling the corridors. We were asked to evacuate to the central courtyard. With quick handshakes and promises to meet again in the Middle East, we filed out. There was no panic evident.

As we moved into the courtyard, many of us looked over our shoulders. We knew two airplanes had hit the World Trade Center—would one strike the Pentagon? The security officials may have shared this concern. In any case, as soon as we reached the open inner courtyard, we were told to evacuate to the south parking lot. As we exited, I saw Pentagon employees assisting tearful colleagues. One woman's mother, working on the custodial force, was unaccounted for.

From the parking lot, we could see the smoke rising from the Pentagon. I, for one, still failed to appreciate the magnitude of the damage and casualties—64 persons aboard the aircraft and 125 inside the Pentagon.[5] Rescue and fire vehicles were flocking to the site. Cell phones were useless, as the system had been swamped with calls. The Metro stop was closed. Streets were quickly shut down so private vehicles could travel only with difficulty. After a long wait, we finally learned that buses would be taking people to nearby Rosslyn where the Metro was still running. I boarded one bus, but the driver could find no way to get there because of the road closures. Instead, we were directed farther and farther west into Virginia. On the bus, people monitored the news via radios. The collapse of the Twin Towers came as a shock. Only then did I fully comprehend the magnitude of the day's attacks. Someone, I presumed al Qaeda's bin Laden, had realized the objective of the 1993 attack, masterminded by Ramzi Yousif: to destroy the towers by collapsing one into the other.[6]

Our bus continued to detour westward until we found ourselves on Lee Highway between Arlington and Falls Church where my family had moved in 1996 from Cairo. I asked to be let off, found a public phone, and called Amal, my wife, who was packing for Yemen. She was only a few minutes away by car. She picked me up, and we spent the rest of the day watching the cascade of events on television.

As with most American families, mine spent the next chaotic days working through our shock. I had escaped unscathed from the Pentagon and reassured my parents without delay. They then had a decision to make. My swearing-in was scheduled for Washington on September 17. With airliners grounded and the nation's capital almost in a state of siege, should they come? My ten siblings from Oregon to Florida and Amal's relatives along the East Coast faced the same dilemma. Would trips across country to one of al Qaeda's target cities make any sense? But by September 17, all but my brother Bob—stuck in Wichita with his two young children—had gathered in the Benjamin Franklin room on the seventh floor of the State Department.

Despite the crushing burdens of 9/11's aftermath, Secretary Powell took time to officiate. He thanked Yemen and its ambassador, Abdulwahab al-Hajri, for a private message of support conveyed to President Bush from Yemeni president Ali Abdullah Saleh. "In return," he continued, "we are giving you support, in terms of providing to the Republic of Yemen one of the finest gentlemen in our service to represent the United States. In Edmund Hull, we are sending the right man, to the right place, at the right time."

My remarks were brief. Counterterrorism was now clearly America's paramount mission. Yemen was an important front, not because it was Osama bin Laden's ancestral homeland, but because al Qaeda had proved its capabilities there in attacking the USS *Cole* and threatening our embassy and investigators. I appreciated the assignment and recalled an Arabic proverb, A change of saddle is as good as a rest (*tibdeel as sarrij fiha raha*).[7]

Secretary Powell graciously greeted the scores of our family members in attendance. My sister Mary, who taught kindergarten in the hamlet of Table Grove, Illinois, presented him with patriotic drawings of support from her students. Not only did he accept them, but in the weeks that followed, the class received a note conveying his warm personal thanks.

Given the circumstances, all was proceeding unusually well—until twenty-four hours before departure. As Amal and I were packing our bags, Brad Hanson, the chargé in Sanaa, and Grant Green, the under secretary for management, introduced "voluntary departure." In view of credible threats to car-bomb the embassy, spouses and children would be allowed to leave post if they desired. Reasonable, it seemed. However, for spouses not already at post, there was nothing voluntary about it. They could not go. Amal was devastated. Born in Jerusalem, she had weathered security crises in Palestine, Egypt, and Tunisia. She had visited Yemen and was quite prepared for its risks as well. We had rented out our house. We had said our good-byes, but now there was one more to be said: to each other. I left for Sanaa alone.

CHAPTER TWO

PARTNER OR TARGET?

International airports are generally the carefully made-up faces that countries present to the outside world. Sanaa's airport was an exception. Stark and utilitarian, it made no pretense of luxury, which exuded from the other capitals of the Arabian Peninsula. Nevertheless, the committee at the foot of the Yemenia Airways Boeing 737 was welcome after the six-hour flight from Frankfurt and the eight-hour one before that from Washington.

The flight had provided me ample time to consider my new assignment. Yemen was an ancient country at the heel of the Arabian Peninsula. In an early period of globalization, it had sat astride the trade routes by which incense moved from its origin in southern Arabia up to Palestine and beyond to Europe, where it was in great demand for religious ceremonies and to perfume the houses of the wealthy. Then Yemen had enjoyed prosperity comparable to that of today's oil states of the Gulf. Great kingdoms had developed during the first millennium BC; the most important centered in Ma'rib in the now remote northeast of Yemen.

After that glory had faded, partly due to the declining use of incense, Yemen built a new reputation in the seventh century as a bastion of the new faith of Islam. The Prophet Mohamed said, "Faith is Yemeni and Wisdom is Yemeni" (*Al iman yamani wa al Hikma yamania*)—a tribute inscribed on Sanaa's public monuments and one often on the lips of the Yemeni people. Yemenis had filled Mohamed's armies. They had also spread as traders and businessmen throughout the Arab world and into Southeast Asia.

One such enterprising family—the bin Ladens—had originated in the Hadramawt, a dramatically fertile valley in the south of Yemen, whose expatriates proved particularly dynamic and astute. Mohammed bin Laden had moved to Saudi Arabia early in the twentieth century and made a fortune in construction contracting. Osama had followed another calling, a personal version of *jihad*, or "holy war." In parallel with the United States, Osama bin Laden had supported the mujahideen in their successful struggle to oust the Soviet Union from Afghanistan in the 1980s. Motivated by faith, family ties, and material rewards, Yemenis had joined that cause in droves. Then many had returned to Yemen. Bin Laden, according to close associates captured by U.S. forces, entertained a similar thought. He married a Yemeni bride and decked himself out in Yemeni attire in so doing. Yemen, with its strong tribes and some remote areas only nominally controlled by the government, was a potential safe haven.[1] I was arriving in Sanaa with a mandate to ensure that did not happen.

Deputy Chief of Mission Brad Hanson was a friendly face at the foot of the disembarkation ladder. I had recruited him only a few months before. He had served previously in Yemen, knew the Yemenis well, and spoke Arabic. Having also been posted to Afghanistan, he was the kind of Foreign Service officer who gravitated to tough assignments. He was soft-spoken and considerate of his staff but hardened and unflinching in crises. I was lucky to have him.

The Ministry of Foreign Affairs protocol representative whisked us through formalities. Luxuries might be lacking, but in their own way Yemenis coddled ambassadors. There was no limousine, however. Substituting for the traditional black Cadillac was a heavily armored Toyota Land Cruiser, the ride of choice in Yemen for terrorists and ambassadors, smugglers and officials.

The American embassy was not far. In the aftermath of the 1984 bombing of our embassy in Beirut, Adm. Bobby Inman, a former director of both the Defense Intelligence Agency and the National Security Agency (NSA), had produced guidelines for American embassies worldwide. At the time, Embassy Sanaa was at the center of the capital, in a compound of traditional stone and brick high-rise structures. With little setback, this site was quickly abandoned, and after painstaking negotiations, a spacious new site was purchased on the northern edge of Sanaa where the Sheraton hotel and the new airport were located.[2] The area had not developed as expected since unification with South Yemen had drawn development to Sanaa's southern suburb of Hadda. Only belatedly had the Sheraton district begun to develop with a new five-star hotel under construction and the Qatari embassy across from it.

The new American embassy presented a formidable appearance. Fronted by a busy four-lane avenue, it was heavily guarded by Central Security Forces (CSF), which answered to the interior minister. The Political Security Organization (PSO) was roughly equivalent to our FBI/CIA, and its agents also kept watch—to protect and to monitor U.S. activity. The embassy's own uniformed local guards manned the huge gate and the cage where vehicles were checked before the delta barriers were lowered, and they were allowed to pass. Once inside, drivers could proceed straight ahead to the chancery or veer left to the residence. The American flag flew from a tall pole that marked the chancery entrance. Large black kites—Yemen's version of America's bald eagles—had built nests in the eucalyptus trees that lined the embassy drives and often soared above the compound, sometimes coming to rest atop that flagpole. The Marine security guard manning the chancery's entrance, called Post One, was another unmistakable sign that you were on American soil, albeit in a foreign land.

The compound was expansive but nearly deserted. The security alert that had prompted the authorized departure of dependents had also resulted in the shutdown of normal embassy operations. But members of our beleaguered regional security office continued to function, as did a large contingent of investigators from the FBI and Naval Criminal Investigation Service (NCIS). Consular business—visas, passports, social security payments, American citizen services—was closed. Political and economic reporting and programs were minimal. Public diplomacy offices were unstaffed.

A sense of paranoia reigned most virulently among the FBI investigators whose work had already revealed troubling connections between the al Qaeda operatives who had successfully attacked the USS *Cole* and Yemeni government officials. Convinced that they were targets, the FBI refused to leave the compound, except to conduct their investigation, and had taken over part of the embassy's small commissary and gym as a dormitory. The FBI identified "enemies" within, too. My predecessor, Amb. Barbara Bodine, had tangled with the legendary John O'Neill, assistant director for the FBI's Counterterrorism Division, because she felt he had conducted himself in high-handed fashion.[3] Asserting an ambassadorial prerogative, she had denied him country clearance.[4] The personal animosity had been grist for the media, including the *Washington Post*. Secretary Powell had not been amused, and easing the strains in the relationship was one of my priorities.

The embassy was blessed with some real counterterrorism talent. The most effective—be they State, FBI, or other agencies—were Arab Americans who often spoke Arabic fluently and had encyclopedic knowledge of al Qaeda and the Yemeni node. These persons also had a knack of winning the trust of their Yemeni counterparts. They included females who provided irrefutable examples of how to function effectively, more so than less capable men, in the most traditional society in the Arab world.

At the center of embassy operations was Sandy Grigola, my secretary. We had worked together for three years in Cairo and were "married" in a professional sense. Sandy managed not only the front office, but also the embassy—with a concern for our mission and the staff, which made her a beloved authority figure. She took as one of her most important responsibilities acquainting the ambassador with his personal shortcomings, but discreetly. If I knew about a family death or a professional disappointment among the staff, it was usually because Sandy's information-gathering was without equal. Her concern extended to the Yemeni employees, and she spent Saturdays teaching young Yemeni women English or introducing new employees to the Suq al Ga', Sanaa's market.[5]

Newly arrived ambassadors quickly signal their priorities and operating style by how they schedule their time. Meetings on security and counterterrorism dominated my first week. On my first day, I convened a general counterterrorism meeting roughly modeled on the CSG meetings that Dick Clarke had used so effectively in Washington. Then I met separately with the FBI/NCIS investigators, counterterrorism experts, and the defense attaché. The following day, I stopped briefly at the Ministry of Foreign Affairs to present copies of my diplomatic credentials and legitimize subsequent activity. Afterward, I headed to PSO headquarters to see Gen. Ghalib Gamish.

General Gamish and I had met the previous March during my visit as chief of S/CT. Slight and balding, he combined a ready smile with an evasive style. For U.S. officials, he had a mixed reputation, but on balance he was thought to be more of a potential partner than adversary. He was clearly an "old school" Yemeni with little formal education and challenging colloquial Arabic. His strength lay in his personal relationship with President Saleh, and I knew he would immediately report to the president that the American ambassador's first substantive call had been to Yemeni intelligence.

My presentation of copies of my credentials meant that I was able to attend the National Day events of September 26. They entailed a long parade of Yemeni security forces at the expansive barracks the Turks had built in Sanaa during their repeated attempts to rule one of the Ottoman Empire's farthest-flung and least governable provinces. President Saleh's speech in Arabic was the main event. I listened to the usual flow of rhetoric celebrating Yemeni independence. Then he turned to contemporary politics. Referring to the recent 9/11 attacks, he said Yemen had itself experienced terrorism and stood with the international coalition in opposing it. Saleh had previously expressed these sentiments in a private letter to President Bush, but I thought it noteworthy that he was reiterating them publicly in an address that Yemeni officials and public would view as policy. I checked my understanding of the president's line with an official of the Foreign Ministry who confirmed it.

Four days later, I was in a position to double-check the president's policy with him personally as I presented my credentials. I noted two signals in the arrangements. First, the relatively brief waiting period in scheduling the formality indicated that Saleh attached particular significance to his relations with Washington. Second, by placing me last at the usually protocol event, he allowed time for a more in-depth talk. I had come prepared. Al Qaeda in Yemen had faces and names, and I intended to focus Saleh on the most important: Abu Ali al-Harithi and Abu Assem al-Mekki.[6] Abu Ali, a Yemeni, was al Qaeda's *amir*, or "prince," in Yemen. Abu Assem al-Mekki, as his name suggested, was a Saudi from Mekka and a facilitator who channeled money to terrorists and their families.[7] They would be the focus of my first and many subsequent meetings with the president.

President Saleh had little patience with ceremony. When I hesitated in presenting my formal credentials and my predecessor's letter of recall, he gestured for me to get on with it. I presented my entourage: my deputy, Brad, as well as the consul and others. Our restricted chat, which followed the formalities, quickly became substantive. Saleh was joined by presidential aides, including Mohamed Suddam, his able interpreter who was also a prominent journalist, and Faris Sanibani, a media adviser who published one of Yemen's English daily newspapers, the *Yemen Observer*.[8] Saleh rarely had ministers attend his meetings. If he needed them, they were a phone call away and always available.

For my part, I wasted no time in pressing my mandate from President Bush to work with Saleh to eliminate al Qaeda's operating base in Yemen. Both our countries had paid dearly. I appreciated President Saleh's declarations—private and now public—in support of the war on terror. We needed to pass from words to deeds. We had identified two key al Qaeda operatives: Abu Ali and Abu Assem. They needed to be captured or killed. To put my extraordinary initial request firmly on the record, I handed him a memo with details of what we would call our high-value targets (HVTs). In response, Saleh voiced reassurance. We agreed that we would establish a special channel for our cooperation on counterterrorism. We parted. I was pleased that I had set a clear objective and test for our counterterrorism relationship.

An ambassador's first duty and profound responsibility is the protection of staff and American citizens in the respective country. In the ambassadorial seminar that prepares first-tour chiefs of mission, political appointees are often taken aback by the directness and challenge of this duty. Any death of an official American or significant damage to the official premises triggers a review in Washington of ambassadorial responsibility and an investigation if there is evidence of dereliction of duty.

The embassy's Emergency Action Committee (EAC) is the official instrument for managing threats. The committee includes virtually all key players from the embassy country team: ambassador, deputy chief of mission, political counselor, defense attaché, regional security officer, consul, and so forth. My EAC met repeatedly in my first weeks in Sanaa to assess threats, primarily kidnapping and vehicle bomb plots against the embassy compound. Our intelligence indicators were "yellow," which meant active plotting but no specifics. We understood that this condition would likely prevail at least until we could kill or capture significant al Qaeda operatives such as Abu Ali al-Harithi and Abu Assem al-Mekki. We could not accomplish that mission, however, without a more fully functioning embassy.

I invited the staff to the residence to get to know one another. Carolina Melara, a recently arrived vice consul, took me aside to say she was deciding whether to curtail her tour. I asked her to delay her decision until I had had a chance to address security issues. Recruiting staff for Sanaa was a nightmare; I could ill afford to lose any more.[9] Shortly thereafter, the acting regional security officer, Chance Rowe, and I took a tour of the compound. He pointed out the many improvements—lighting, barriers, and so forth—that he had personally made.[10] Others were pending: most notably, concertina wire needed to be placed atop the relatively low perimeter wall, and the grill façade in front of the embassy needed to be replaced with a closed wall. My predecessor had objected to these projects lest the embassy come to resemble a fort. I took another tack and approved them immediately. Security trumps image. Few factors complicate a terrorist's planning more than constantly changing security arrangements at its target. Make that target hard enough, and the terrorist will choose an easier one. Moreover, Yemen was a country where insecurity was historic. Tribal sheikhs and villagers traditionally located their houses on high, often nearly inaccessible ground. They then fortified them with walls and towers. A fortified American embassy kept with Yemeni tradition, not violated it.[11]

At the same time, Secretary Powell's injunction not to allow terrorists to cause us to retreat to bunkers had to be followed. I set up an early, very public tour of old

Sanaa, including its historic gate Bab al-Yemen, central mosque, and library. My thirty years in the Middle East had made it easy for me to appreciate the significance of the library's greatest treasure: a Koran donated by Ali, the prophet's nephew and an early khalifa, or "successor."

I also explored Yemen's tribal traditions. In the north, two great tribal federations—the Bakil and the Hashid—held sway. The former was more numerous, but the latter was better organized. President Saleh was a Hashid, but he was not first in that tribe's hierarchy. That honor was Sheikh Abdullah al-Ahmar's, who combined his status with his positions as speaker of the parliament and leader of the Islamic opposition party, Islah.

Driving into Sheikh al-Ahmar's compound was similar to entering a "state within a state." Tribal guards mingled with the official security forces whose tribal loyalties were far stronger than civic ones. The sheikh was immaculately dressed in tribal robes and wearing a spectacular *jambiyya*—reported to be worth $10,000.[12] Prominently displayed in his hall was a mother-of-pearl model of the Dome of the Rock, the major Islamic shrine in Jerusalem's Old City.[13]

I genuinely respected the sheikh and knew he had much to teach me about Yemen. Employing my somewhat rusty Arabic, I asked about relations between the tribes and the state. He dismissed any conflict of interest.

"Yemenis are tribesmen. Tribesmen are Yemenis," he said.

I asked what the tribes' priorities were.

"Roads, hospitals, schools, jobs," he replied.

So far, so good. I then ventured into dangerous territory. I noted that the Yemeni custom of chewing khat struck me as a serious impediment to development and a health risk to its consumers. Chewing the new leaves of the khat tree is an ancient Yemeni tradition. Yemenis rush through their main noon meal, usually *salta*, a hearty stew, to relax with friends often in rooftop aeries where they chew the leaves, drink hot tea, and converse on all things of import, including politics and poetry. It is late afternoon before a state of bliss (*kayf*) is reached, and the Yemenis then return to their shops, which are open late into the night.[14]

The sheikh disagreed. Khat was benign and had the salutary economic effect of re-cycling money from the relatively rich cities to the relatively poor countryside. I demurred and, citing President Saleh's public admonishment to eschew chewing, said that I would not chew khat during my tenure in Yemen.[15]

We parted, agreeing to disagree on khat. With pleasure I noted in the following day's newspapers prominent reporting of my meeting with the sheikh and visit to the mosque. Where previously I was only a new ambassador interacting with "official" Yemen, now I had signaled interest and sympathy for Yemen's long history, Islam, and the tribes. Although the Yemenis could not be expected to deal with me as a complex personality, I could consciously invent a simplified persona to which they could relate.

As mentioned earlier, an ambassador's charge extends beyond the embassy to encompass all American citizens in that country. This responsibility was especially challenging in Yemen because we estimated that nearly thirty thousand Yemenis enjoyed American citizenship. The vast majority were hard workers who had done well in the United States and had then returned to Yemen to live in relative comfort on modest pensions and Social Security.[16] To connect with this constituency, we scheduled a "town hall" meeting. With several days' notice, Americans from many parts of Yemen, particularly the central district of Ib, showed up. Chance, our acting regional security officer, was not happy. The residence's *mafraj* overflowed with Yemenis in traditional garb, including jambiyyas.[17] As was the custom, shoes were removed at the entrance and piled chaotically.

I felt curiosity, but no animosity, from the assembled and weighed in. One of the first questions had an edge, however. The international media was reporting that Yemen was a possible "target" in the international "War on Terror."[18] Did the United States intend to attack Yemen? I realized my answer would be the meeting's headline and had also heard President Saleh publicly and privately enlist in the war on terror. A word for a word seemed appropriate.

"Yemen is a partner, not a target in the war on terror," I said. Then I explained how Yemeni and U.S. interests coincided, and noted President Saleh's commitment. My job would be translating that commitment into action serving those interests.

Both international and local media reported the formulation.[19] Saber-rattling continued from some circles in Washington, but I received no rebuke from my bosses.

Washington was focusing on Yemen, however. In my predeparture rounds, I had included meetings at the NSC with Zal Khalilzad and Gen. Wayne Downing.[20] Khalilzad was senior director for the Near East and South Asia, and General Downing had inherited Dick Clarke's counterterrorism responsibilities. From my own service on the NSC from 1990 to 1992, I knew that a country stood a much better chance of garnering attention if both a functional office and a regional one took an interest. I also knew that the White House priority would be on Afghanistan, where al Qaeda camps were churning out thousands of terrorists, but that someone needed to attack al Qaeda nodes elsewhere as well. The United States could not do it all nor do it effectively itself everywhere.

Yemen was a key node. In some way, all recent al Qaeda successes—the attacks against our East African embassies, the attack on the *Cole*, and even 9/11—were linked to al Qaeda operatives in Yemen. With U.S. priorities radically shifted to counterterrorism, a Washington visit by Saleh was suddenly a possibility.

The invitation came via Deputy Assistant Secretary Ryan Crocker in State's Bureau of Near Eastern Affairs (NEA).[21] Nothing formal—a secure telephone call. The problem was the proposed date: November 27. It fell in the middle of Ramadan, the Muslim month of fasting.

Saleh was affronted by the timing and asked that it be rescheduled in December, after Ramadan. Ryan confirmed to me that, with holidays and other presidential commitments, the Ramadan date was "take it or leave it." I prevailed upon Saleh to take it, and he did.

He then provided a challenge on another front. After meeting with tribal leaders to explain his new policy for combating terrorism, Saleh called me late at night to plead for a dramatic increase in U.S. economic assistance targeted at the remote areas of Ma'rib, Al Jawf, and Shabwah. Along with Abyan in the south, these areas were the country's wildest. The tribes were strong; government control was tenuous at best. Key al Qaeda operatives were located there. I was sympathetic to the president's request and undertook to see what could be done.

Countering terrorism had long seemed to me a campaign that went far beyond intelligence and security. In many ways, it resembled counterinsurgency, success of which depended primarily on winning the hearts and minds of the population. An essential part of our effort would be capturing or killing al Qaeda operatives, but that would be difficult if they enjoyed the support of the local population. Moreover, eliminated terrorists could be quickly replaced unless the general population was turned against al Qaeda. We would have to use the entire tool kit: diplomacy to create political will, intelligence to locate targets and defend ourselves, security or military forces to capture or kill the operatives, economic assistance and public diplomacy to win popular support. In this context, Saleh's pressure to address the needs of Yemen's deprived areas was not a distraction but a key element in successful counterterrorism strategy.

I began a crash course on Yemen's tribes, focusing on Ma'rib,[22] and quickly realized that the governor was a major part of the problem. Previously banished from the capital for maintaining private prisons, he was now mismanaging Ma'rib. As governor, he possessed powers and responsibilities that were vast and included security and development. I saw the current situation as a vicious circle: bad governance, insecurity, national and international neglect, lack of development. I then constructed a theoretic virtuous circle in its stead: good governance, enhanced security, national and international support, local development. I was careful to include no specific dollar amounts of assistance.

In my view, there was no reason why the United States alone should foot the bill. European countries had long-standing interests in Yemen. For the Dutch, Yemen had been one of the countries where they had concentrated economic assistance with the intent of making their limited means produce a significant effect. The Germans also had historic ties with Yemen that dated from the activities of their scholars, such as Carsten Niebuhr in the eighteenth century, and orientalists. The Japanese had an active and well-funded program in Yemen, although tribal kidnappings had placed many of their efforts on hold. The British were right-minded, but London was providing few resources. The French were blasé, while the Italians were potentially interested as Yemen was a relatively popular tourist destination.

The Japanese ambassador, Yuichi Ishii Oki, hosted a dinner and invited me to present my thoughts. I brought a PowerPoint presentation of "Plan Ma'rib" and made my case. Engaged in an archaeological excavation in Ma'rib, the Germans welcomed more interest but noted security concerns. Their nationals had been subjected to intimidation and even kidnappings. It was a rough neighborhood.

I needed a reality check from the Yemeni side. The best bet was Abdulkarim al-Iryani. Probably the smartest man in Yemen, al-Iryani was slight of stature but a formidable politician. He was among a remarkable cadre of senior Yemeni officials educated in the United States on USAID programs in the 1950s.[23] Earning a PhD in biology from Yale University, he returned to Sanaa and carved out a distinguished career: minister of education, foreign minister, prime minister, and currently secretary-general of the ruling party. His family had provided judges and scholars to Yemen for centuries, and he discussed Yemeni history and Islamic questions as almost family affairs. His village—Al Iryan—continued to provide some of Yemen's, and therefore the world's, best coffee.

Noting President Saleh's late-night request, I proceeded to outline my plan and showed al-Iryani an Arabic version of the PowerPoint with the vicious and virtuous circles. He expressed interest and asked for copies, which I provided. For his part, he focused on Saleh's upcoming visit to Washington. He proposed that this visit culminate with the signing of a memorandum that would place Yemeni-U.S. counterterrorism cooperation on a firm footing. I agreed to try my hand while I was awaiting feedback on Plan Ma'rib. I subsequently passed him a very general draft and e-mailed both documents to the State Department for feedback as well.

In Sanaa, as in all of the Islamic world, Friday brought both communal prayers at noon and the weekend. I had taken to spending part of mine at the Equestrian Club, owned by a son of Abdullah al-Ahmar, where I was acquainting myself with the ill-trained but beautiful Arabian horses of Yemen. I enjoyed the physical challenge but was also aware of two political messages I was sending. I was relating to the fact that the horse was the symbol of the ruling party while demonstrating openness to a family enterprise of the opposition's leader. While in transit dressed for riding, I was summoned to the presidential palace by cell phone. A late morning Friday call was highly unusual. I quickly returned to the embassy for suitable attire.

When I arrived at the Presidency, Saleh was livid. Who did I think I was? Yemen had shed blood to end the British occupation of Aden. It would not accept a new "high commissioner" in the guise of an American ambassador. He stopped short, just short it seemed of declaring me persona non grata.

This was strong stuff for a newly minted ambassador. Not an initial stumble on unfamiliar ground, but potentially a plunge into a diplomatic abyss. And I did not even know how I had offended him.

Plan Ma'rib, he continued, had been considered by the cabinet and had caused an uproar. My proposal for a treaty to combat counterterrorism was similarly offensive and rejected.

Finally, it dawned on me. My friend Abdulkarim al-Iryani had passed along both Plan Ma'rib and the draft memorandum to the president who had then presented them formally to the Yemeni government. I was receiving feedback at deafening decibels.

Saleh vented and vented. When finally he felt that he had reestablished the proper relationship between head of state and envoy, he allowed me to respond. Plan Ma'rib, I explained, was his idea. He had phoned me to request assistance. I had designed a plan and was merely seeking Yemeni reaction. It was not designed to go to the government as a whole, but to him alone through a trusted channel. The memorandum was also a Yemeni idea from our good friend and his adviser Abdulkarim. If he found it problematic, then I would immediately abandon the effort.

Mollified, Saleh reassessed. On second thought, the memorandum might be useful. He would direct his chief of staff to pursue it. Plan Ma'rib was another matter. Any suggestion that the problems of the deprived areas stemmed from bad governance was entirely unacceptable.

I left the "woodshed" chagrined and began projecting my time in Yemen in months, not years. I consoled myself by remembering that there were respectable ambassadorial precedents. George Kennan had fallen afoul of Soviet authorities five months into his tenure in Moscow. A legend in the Near East bureau, Dick Parker had been sent packing by King Hassan II of Morocco immediately after he had been sent to Blair House, where the king was staying during an early visit to Washington, to correct a misperception. In my own experience, I recalled that the ambassador to Cairo, Nick Veliotes, had been the sacrificial victim following the *Achille Lauro* affair when, in 1985, U.S. Air Force planes had intercepted and forced down an Egyptair flight carrying terrorists working for Abu Abbas. I would have distinguished company in my disgrace.

Life went on. Acceptance of an abbreviated tenure can be liberating and a spur. Two areas benefited. First, Rear Adm. Bert Calland, responsible for special operations in the Central Command, visited in late October and brought with him a navy SEAL's determination and commitment. In Calland and his successors, I found ideal partners in addressing the security dimension of countering terrorism in Yemen. We had no plan at this stage, but we shared a mission.

I also received an invitation from the *Yemen Times*, a leading English-language newspaper, to address a colloquium on U.S.-Yemeni relations. At the event, the urbane Foreign Minister Abu Bakr al-Qirby provided a lucid history of the relationship, which I found personally instructive. It was always useful to place oneself in another's shoes and see how matters appeared. For my part, I simply introduced myself, noting that I had ten siblings and therefore came from a respectably sized "tribe." I noted Yemen's photogenic beauty, friendly people, rich culture, and long history. Then I told of a trip to the nearby town of Thula. There, I had spoken in Arabic with an ordinary soldier who had independently articulated President Saleh's policy that Yemen must counter terrorism because it is a victim of terrorism. I had also met an enterprising teenager, Fatima, who complained that there were no tourists to buy her headscarves. I had been thinking about the challenges confronting Yemen and wanted to propose a hypothesis—*La tanmiya bidoun al amn wa la amn bidoun al tanmiya* (No development without security, and no security without development). Security included an end to the kidnapping of foreigners, which was crippling tourism and international development efforts. Also, security meant an end to the presence of al Qaeda.

Development had to reach the deprived areas: Ma'rib, Al Jawf, and Shabwah. Their strong tribes would need to support it. There was a desire to do so. I had heard it from tribal leaders, including Sheikh Abdullah al-Ahmar, as well as from students, teachers, and local officials. Good governors made a great difference; we would support them. The international community had neglected Yemen. No country could be left behind lest terrorists take advantage. Bringing security and development to Yemen was the strategic challenge facing U.S.-Yemeni relations.

The next edition of the *Yemen Times* duly noted the colloquium and headlined what it found newsworthy: "American Ambassador Visits *Yemen Times* Editorial Offices." I was surprised and disappointed. The foreign minister's analysis and mine were not trivial. They represented where the relationship had been and where I thought it needed to go. Yemen's leading journalists had reduced the event to protocol. Unfortunately, I had no American public diplomacy staff on which to draw. Security-driven departures and recruitment failings had left the embassy in its own vicious circle. I instructed the embassy's Yemeni staff to convey my disappointment. I moved public diplomacy up a notch on the to-do list.

Another to-do was human rights. I personally disagreed with the all-too-common dichotomy of counterterrorism and human rights. If counterterrorism resembles counterinsurgency as essentially a battle for "hearts and minds," then any strategy that neglects human rights risks alienation of the populace. In Yemen I found a likely ally—and an unlikely one. The former was Far'a Wahba, the only woman in Yemen's cabinet and the newly created minister for human rights. I met her in early November and found her impressive. Dr. Wahba was a splendid role model and deeply committed to a realistic program that would improve human rights in Yemen. Human rights activists in Yemen had a love-hate reaction to the State Department's annual report on human rights. They resented judgments by a government that they saw as complicit in denying human rights to the Palestinians. They also acknowledged many shortcomings in their society and welcomed international attention.

The latter sat in the Ministry of the Interior. Dr. Rashad al-Alimi was unlike any interior minister whom I had met in thirty years in the Middle East. A professor of sociology, he was an expert on Yemen's tribes and tribal law. His English was rudimentary, but his Arabic was elegant, and he patiently suffered mine. He was as formidable as a manager as he was ambitious to improve Yemeni security forces and extend their sway. He was the protector of foreign embassies and foreigners. We had much to discuss and many mutual services to render. He was also a surprise. As we concluded our talk on security and terrorism, he asked to raise a last issue: human rights. In terms worthy of a Princeton professor, he proceeded to analyze the connection between counterterrorism and human rights, to note that he was actively collaborating with Dr. Far'a and to welcome embassy attention. He shared with me a wise motto, *Rahimallah emra 'an ahda 'elaiya 'oyobi* (God bless the one who points out my shortcomings). Words, I knew, did not equate to deeds. Security forces would be prone to excesses under any management. Nevertheless, I had only expected an ally on counterterrorism and was delighted to find one on human rights as well.

Meanwhile, Ramadan had arrived. Ordinary business was put aside while Yemenis fasted from sunup until sundown and feasted thereafter. President Saleh's trip to Washington impended. For a brief moment, Washington was focused on Yemen. It was a precious opportunity, so I sent in a cable titled, "Saleh Visit and Counterterrorism: Moving from Words to Deeds." I proposed three objectives:

1. Confirming Saleh's "strategic choice" to support the international counterterrorism coalition
2. Concluding the memorandum to translate this commitment into a "comprehensive counterterrorism strategy with practical steps"
3. Agreeing on priority steps to eliminate al Qaeda's leadership in Yemen

In the midst of Operation Enduring Freedom in Afghanistan, I noted the importance of preempting any attempt by al Qaeda to substitute Yemen for Afghanistan. I described al Qaeda's presence in five governorates: Ma'rib, Shabwah, Al Jawf, Amran, and Khawlan. I reminded Washington of how al Qaeda had used Yemeni operating space to support the attacks on our embassies in East Africa, the *Cole*, the World Trade Center, and the Pentagon. I reiterated Saleh's verbal commitments and pressed to formalize them in the Iryani-proposed memorandum, which would include enhanced Anti-Terrorism Assistance (ATA) funds and Terrorist Interdiction Program (TIP) funds.[24] Finally, I noted the recent visit by Admiral Calland and the incipient military-to-military cooperation.

In theory, all this made eminent sense—at least to its proponent. In practice, major problems had arisen. The memorandum was never meant to be a legal commitment, but rather a political one by each country's leader. It should have galvanized

Yemeni political will and legitimized cooperation with U.S. counterparts. On the U.S. side, it should have made Yemen a presidential priority in the war on terror.

Saleh passed this memorandum to his chief of staff who proceeded to involve Yemeni lawyers. The Yemenis sought to include extravagant dollar commitments and dilute their specific commitments. Meanwhile, in Washington, Mike Miller, our intrepid desk officer in the State Department, tried his best but made little headway on the memorandum. Plan Ma'rib fared no better. I had learned from Dick Clarke that no counterterrorism program is serious without resources and from Mike Sheehan to be bold. Therefore, for Washington's consideration only, I had attached a $200 million target for a multiyear program. A great deal of money admittedly, but the NEA had annually requested more that $4 billion to support the Middle East peace process. If we were serious about a war on terror, then should we not be willing to spend hundreds of millions? After several frustrating sessions with the Yemeni lawyers on the memorandum, I left Sanaa with a text acceptable to me. I would have to see for myself what support I could muster in Washington for funding the Yemen front of the war on terror.

CHAPTER THREE

A MEETING OF MINDS

Counterterrorism is the preeminent interagency issue. Appropriately, the NSC meeting to prepare for the visit of President Saleh was the policy focal point. Unfortunately, the meeting would bring together a group of relative strangers with clashing agendas, limited authorities, and little preparation time. It was a recipe for failure.

There was another way to do this, exemplified by Dick Clarke and his management of CSG. Before 9/11 and in the following months, Dick had formed by force of personality a group of experts from various agencies who shared a common mission: to combat the increasing threat of terrorism. Clarke was himself a strong personality and widely disliked for his bulldozing, intimidating style. In the State Department, he was particularly unpopular. State's Foreign Service officers spend about half their careers overseas and learn to value bilateral relationships. Dick was a creature of Washington—DoD, State, but mostly the NSC—and generally he saw bilateral relations as purely a means to the end of U.S. interests as defined by Dick Clarke.[1] Dick's CSG was not a collection of sycophants. Other powerful personalities, such as the FBI's John O'Neill and Dale Watson, CIA's Cofer Black, and State's Mike Sheehan, disagreed vigorously and protected their bureaucratic turf. To a remarkable extent, however, they did share an overriding counterterrorism priority and battled to promote this priority within their home agencies.

Clarke and his CSG were now history. The interagency meeting to discuss President Saleh's visit was chaired by the regional senior director, Zal Khalilzad, with the NSC's counterterrorism office represented by its deputy, John Craig, former ambassador to Oman, Yemen's neighbor to the east. As director of Arabian Peninsula affairs in State, Craig had a history with Yemen and its president. Like O'Neill, he also had a history with my strong-willed predecessor, Barbara Bodine. Neither disposed him to cooperation with Sanaa's ruler or with the U.S. ambassador in Sanaa. Negotiating a memorandum text with the Yemenis had been a painful exercise in reinforcing strong general commitments while avoiding premature financial ones. However, the NSC meeting led to a bureaucratic dead end because some in Washington were not even ready for general commitments. For them, Yemen was a "target," not a "partner."

How to explain this view to President Saleh, who was resting comfortably at the Ritz-Carlton, Washington? I did not have long to consider the matter as I was summoned in short order to meet with him. He preempted with his own surprise. He would not sign the memorandum; rather he proposed that Foreign Minister al-Qirby do so with Secretary Powell. Yemen's constitution and legal system so dictated, he claimed.

Neither for the first time nor the last, the president's machinations provided a relatively graceful exit from an awkward diplomatic situation. I had only to resist his last-minute change and play for time, and the memorandum would succumb to a natural bureaucratic death with minimal recriminations. Saleh would continue to pursue his preferred approach in the Washington meetings but, confronted with suspicions and indifference, made no headway. Our backing away was far from an ideal solution because it fed Yemeni suspicions in turn. It was left to see whether high-level personal contact could establish a basis for cooperation that had eluded lower-level bureaucrats.

Saleh's meetings with the principals of the Bush administration were a mixed bag. As an ambassador, I needed a meeting of the minds on the critical issue of terrorism. CIA director George Tenet did the best at laying this foundation. He was focused and well briefed. His message was simple and consistent. The United States needed to see results from Saleh's verbal commitment to partnership, and then it would provide tangible resources.

FBI director Bob Mueller was similarly focused on terrorism but primarily in the context of the ongoing USS *Cole* investigation. Although the president had radically shifted U.S. priorities in the wake of 9/11 from prosecution of terrorists to prevention of terrorist attacks, the FBI's interest in successful prosecutions proved enduring. Still, Mueller's personal commitment to a partnership with a cooperative Yemen was impressive. On the *Cole* case, the director asked for patience in not rushing to trial until the investigation had exhausted all leads.

For Secretary of Defense Rumsfeld, Saleh put protocol aside and called at the Pentagon, the scene of one of the 9/11 attacks. Unlike in the previous meetings, the secretary of defense had been poorly briefed by his staff. A generally amicable meeting ran aground when Rumsfeld began to push Saleh for a speedy trial of the *Cole* suspects. Of course, the Yemeni president had just heard the opposite appeal from the director of the FBI and was naturally confused. As the only U.S. representative at all meetings, I had to correct the secretary and succinctly explain our overriding interest in a full investigation that would uncover as much of al Qaeda's network as possible. Rumsfeld took the correction in stride, and I never felt any personal resentment.

President Saleh's meeting with Secretary Powell was cordial—almost too cordial. Saleh used the occasion to press his case on both the Palestinian issue and Iraq. His points were reasonable, but we wasted precious time on issues in which Yemen was marginal to Washington. The core concern of ending al Qaeda's sanctuary in Yemen went insufficiently addressed. From my perspective, we faced a completely counterproductive outcome from his visit. I might return to Sanaa as ambassador accountable for U.S. efforts to end the Palestinian-Israeli conflict or for a peaceful resolution of our differences with Iraq.

Therefore, a great deal rested on the concluding meeting in the Oval Office with President Bush. Fortunately, Bruce Riedel, my former colleague from the NSC and now senior director for the Near East, arranged for a prebriefing of President Bush. We had barely five minutes, but it proved sufficient. As Bruce and I entered the room, we found both Powell and Rice had preceded us. The president bolted from his desk and asked what the United States wanted from Yemen. The others turned to me as the administration's man in Sanaa. I told the president that Saleh was primed to be helpful and that we needed to direct that willingness to specific objectives, particularly the capture or killing of al Qaeda's leadership in Yemen, Abu Ali and Abu Assem. The president himself maintained photo arrays of key al Qaeda operatives and could appreciate such a direct approach. Bruce helpfully warned that the president should preempt. Saleh's last Oval Office meeting with Clinton had gone nowhere because Saleh had been allowed to begin and had filibustered for nearly the entire meeting.

In the event, the president performed impressively. He laid out the common ground available for a U.S.-Yemeni counterterrorism partnership. Saleh, who both understood and appreciated straightforwardness, pronounced himself committed to such a partnership. I felt I had clear and actionable agreement at the very top. Doubts, some at very high levels, remained, but at least the United States would for the present treat Yemen as a partner, not a target.

Before leaving Washington, I made a few last calls, including one to Under Secretary Marc Grossman, one of our generation's most brilliant diplomats. Marc and I had worked together as staff aides in the NEA bureau during the long, painful year following the taking of our colleagues as hostages in Tehran. More than anyone else, as director general of the Foreign Service, he was responsible for my appointment to Sanaa. He asked how the Oval Office meeting went. I briefed him on the apparent meeting of minds, but I also noted the deep skepticism around town that Saleh would act.

Marc aptly summed up my situation: "You need scalps."

CHAPTER FOUR

GROWING PAINS

On his way back to Yemen, President Saleh stopped over in Europe. Paris and Berlin were favorite destinations where he was always well received. Generally, the Europeans provided less material support but did so more graciously and therefore earned ample diplomatic rewards. In this instance, however, Berlin proved an embarrassment. While enjoying German hospitality, the president was informed that the German manager of the Mercedes-Benz dealership in Sanaa had been kidnapped. The kidnappers were four young men from a Khawlan tribe, notorious for such activities. They had no association with al Qaeda and sought a material, not political, payoff.

Kidnapping in Yemen has a long history. Hostages play a role in tribal law as pledges of good behavior. Their captors generally treat them well and return them once satisfied.[1] This tradition had engendered many jokes about hostages returning from captivity lavishly fed and delighted by the experience. Some observers have argued almost seriously that it is a unique form of Yemeni tourism.

In 1998 the practice turned nasty. The Islamic Army of Aden, led by Zein al-Abdine al-Mihdar and inspired by a radical Egyptian sheikh in London named Abu Hamza al-Masri, kidnapped twelve British, two Australian, and two American tourists in late December near Mudiyah in southern Yemen.[2] Al-Mihdar demanded the release of nine jailed Islamists and the lifting of United Nations sanctions on Iraq. A Yemeni tradition had evolved into a twentieth-century terrorist act. Yemen's security forces responded forcefully. In their operation, four of the tourists—three British and one Australian—were killed.[3] Al-Mihdar was captured, tried, convicted, and executed. The

Yemeni government demanded the extradition of al-Masri, and there ensued a long diplomatic exchange with the British government to build a legal case on which to do so. Some of al-Mihdar's associates were British nationals found guilty and imprisoned. Yemeni justice failed European standards, so the British ambassador in Sanaa was periodically required by London to protest their captivity and press for release. The Yemenis received, as well as gave, mixed signals on terrorism.

I saw the "tribal" kidnappings as a slippery slope into the potential abyss of terrorist ones. Within the American embassy, we regularly discussed kidnappings in our EAC. Embassy staff regularly reported surveillance, and in one case a probable abduction was thwarted by the young officer's savvy maneuvering to reach a friend's house. The State Department had placed Sanaa on "authorized departure" status, partially as a result of the continuing kidnapping threat, which meant we could not recruit staff effectively.

U.S. counterterrorism policy strictly forbade the American government making any substantive concessions to kidnappers.[4] Our allies generally took softer lines. Any country with a reputation for paying ransom found its nationals were fair game throughout the Middle East and Central Asia. In Yemen one Asian country's development program was curtailed by the peril of its experts. Once again, a vicious circle prevailed with insecurity and underdevelopment reinforcing each other.

The kidnappers of the Mercedes-Benz manager had erred in their timing, however. Saleh was embarrassed. He ordered a firm response, and Yemeni security forces encircled the kidnappers. Accounts of the subsequent events varied. The official Yemeni account claimed their forces liberated the German. The hostage himself reported to the German ambassador that he managed to wander away from his captors in the night and found Yemeni security forces who then took him to safety. In any case, Yemeni security forces arrested three of the four kidnappers, who were tried, convicted, and imprisoned.[5]

Applauding Saleh's firmness, I began my rounds of introductory calls and gave priority to the tribal sheikhs rather than to the political party leaders.[6] I reasoned that al Qaeda's strategy was not to play Yemen's political game, but to establish support among the fiercely independent tribes, especially in remote areas. My Arabic proved helpful since I could relate directly. In my initial calls upon Yemen's tribal sheikhs, I pushed for them to follow Saleh's lead on kidnappings. "No development without security; no security without development" continued to be my overall mantra. On December 10, I met with Sheikh Naji al-Shayf, the paramount sheikh of the Bakil tribe to praise him personally for taking a public stand against kidnapping.

For his part, Saleh was following up on his Washington trip. On December 1, soon after his return to Sanaa, he called together in Al Hudaydah a meeting of political and tribal notables to explain his visit and put forward a more aggressive counterterrorism policy. Yemen was a victim of terrorism and "opposed terrorism in all its forms whoever commits it."[7] Saleh pledged publicly to capture and interrogate suspected terrorists but rejected outside intervention in addressing Yemen's terrorist problem. He also strongly condemned kidnapping of foreigners.

Yemeni security forces also took down Ahmed al-Hadda's house, which had been identified as a terrorist logistic center. Its telephone number—200 578—had gained notoriety throughout the FBI. The link connecting the East Africa bombings, the USS Cole, and 9/11 was severed, but the operation provided little useful intelligence.[8]

Saleh soon made a down payment on his Oval Office commitment. He summoned me to the Ministry of Defense for a meeting, not in its war room but rather in a gazebo in its courtyard. Saleh said negotiations were under way to bring about Abu Ali and Abu Assem's surrender. If not successful within two days, Yemeni security forces would launch an operation. Locating Abu Ali, at least, was not difficult. He was comfortably ensconced in his compound in Shabwah, near Ma'rib. Abu Assem had also been located near Ma'rib, in Husn al-Jallal. Saleh requested body armor for the strike force.

In the Middle East, it is usually a mistake to take any temporal estimate too seriously. In Cairo as a young diplomat, I had been told of a dictum of a well-seasoned British counterpart: "Any action will take twice as long as you expect, but you will also find that you have twice the time you thought you had to accomplish it." In this case, the Yemeni military forces needed eight days before launching their operation. Still, when we received word on December 17 that forces were moving toward the remote locations, we were encouraged.

A fiasco ensued on December 18. The Yemeni military units conducting the operations included armored personnel carriers, so surprise was impossible. Abu Ali had slipped away. The Yemeni security forces asked to search the compound and were accorded the privilege. Nothing. Matters were much worse in the Husn al-Jallal operation, which had been added at the last minute. Given that Abu Assem was from Saudi Arabia and without strong Yemeni tribal ties, the operation should have been easier. Distrust between the tribes and the government was acute, however. While a search of the compound was under negotiation, a Yemeni Air Force jet flew over and broke the sound barrier. Reacting, the heavily armed tribesmen opened fire on the Yemeni security forces, and nineteen officers and soldiers were killed. Twenty-eight, mostly security personnel, were injured. A number of military vehicles were also destroyed.[9] Abu Assem, of course, was long gone.

The news plunged the embassy's counterterrorism team into a deep depression. An opportunity to decapitate al Qaeda in Yemen had been lost. Yemeni security forces had failed, and failed badly. Al Qaeda's leadership was now alert and hiding in Yemen's vast, rugged, and tribal hinterland. Yemen's armed forces had been embarrassed and intimidated. There was a long, long road ahead.

Washington reacted differently. Because we had been informed before the operation, the U.S. government had been paying attention, and the American media was attentive as well after the fact.[10] Both State and NSC staff called to inform me that President Bush had been briefed. Saleh's determination to act was seen as more significant than the failure of his security forces to perform. Yemeni blood had symbolically redeemed Saleh's Oval Office pledge. In Yemen political will plus practical capability equaled effective counterterrorism. For the moment at least, we had half the equation's elements.

CENTCOM, whose area of military operations includes the Middle East, did not wait for Washington to make up its mind before escalating the engagement. I had met CENTCOM's commander, Gen. Tommy Franks, at his headquarters in Tampa before leaving for Yemen. I found him to be not only a formidable soldier but also, in his own West Texas manner, a formidable diplomat. We agreed quickly that Yemen was a critical al Qaeda node and we had to do more. He was particularly interested in training the Yemeni special forces, commanded by President Saleh's son Ahmed. In Jordan the late King Hussein had groomed his son similarly, and King Abdullah had become a strong U.S. ally in the war on terror.

Rear Adm. Bert Calland, CENTCOM's lead on counterterrorism, had visited Yemen in late October. He was now on the phone to discuss developments. We agreed that Saleh had demonstrated his political will in the Ma'rib operations, and the Yemenis should now receive training and possibly support. What CENTCOM had in mind followed the Afghanistan model: AC-130 gunships to soften a target prior to Yemeni forces taking it. In military parlance, this was one of many "kinetic" options. There would be no problem funding such an operation. DoD effectively had a blank check for kinetic options. Training the Yemenis was problematic, however. Funds were limited, and Yemen technically did not qualify as a formal member of the Operation Enduring Freedom coalition.[11]

The State Department and NSC wrestled with the policy. During Saleh's visit, the Washington bureaucracy had deadlocked on "target versus partner." His actions since the visit, particularly the Ma'rib operation, had temporarily at least strengthened those who favored partnership, including me. Under Secretary of State Marc Grossman's deft hand was steering the issue through Washington's treacherous policymaking process. Skeptics, particularly NSC's John Craig, remained. Tactically, it is almost always easier to thwart policy initiatives than to accomplish them. Grossman asked that the embassy send in its analysis, including how Yemen differed from Afghanistan. The trick would be to move the United States to active partnership but not to kinetic options envisioned by some in CENTCOM.

As Saleh had taken more time than I had expected in mounting the Ma'rib operation, Washington would take more time than expected in making its policy. The immediate decision, in fact, was to send Assistant Secretary Bill Burns to Yemen to assess further. From my perspective, his visit was a positive step. He had credibility in Washington and acute sensitivity across cultures. A former ambassador to Jordan, he had helped engineer CENTCOM's successful engagement with Jordanian special forces.

Bill arrived January 17 in Sanaa. Our brief for him focused on the Ma'rib operation and why it had misfired. Defense Attaché Bob Newman graphically explained how difficult it was for Yemeni security forces to pursue Abu Ali and Abu Assem in the remote, rugged terrain of Ma'rib and Al Jawf. Bill quickly absorbed the "ground truth."

Since it was January, Saleh had moved to the southern port city of Aden, where he spent a part of each year. Formerly the capital of South Yemen, Aden was deemed the commercial capital of Yemen. It had no less political significance. His presence represented both Yemen's success in expelling the British from a former crown colony, and North Yemen's success in defeating the Marxists of South Yemen and uniting the country.[12] Generally, southerners were better educated and often resented northern political dominance. Saleh had shrewdly enlisted such southerners as Prime Minister Abdul Qader Bajammal and Foreign Minister Abu Bakr al-Qirby into his government. Aden itself, however, was languishing under a long-serving incompetent governor.

From Sanaa to Aden, it took a day by road and an hour by air. Unfortunately, Yemenia Airways had no flights convenient for Bill's meeting. The president graciously offered his personal helicopter, which gave us an additional hour to discuss the upcoming meeting.[13] I reiterated Bruce Riedel's counsel to seize the initiative lest our discussion veer into a presidential discourse on Palestine, Iraq, or Afghanistan. Bill had another, more mundane but pressing concern. He was scheduled to meet Saudi princes early that evening. If the meeting with Saleh ran long, he would miss his flight connection and offend the Saudis. On the way into Saleh's guesthouse overlooking Aden Port, we mentioned Bill's predicament to the presidential protocol officials. If necessary, could they hold the commercial flight from Sanaa to Riyadh, so Bill could make it? They were noncommittal.

Saleh was pleased to see Bill, whom he respected highly. For his part, Bill gracefully preempted. He welcomed the chance to discuss a wide range of issues with the president but needed first to convey regards and a letter from President Bush. Bill then outlined the essence of an understanding on counterterrorism that tracked the intent of the aborted memorandum of understanding. In response, President Saleh promised "no reverse, no retreat" in efforts to eradicate al Qaeda's presence in Yemen, "regardless of political pressures, tribal pressures, or extremist pressures." Yemen had sealed its commitment in blood. The meeting concluded: Saleh had his presidential commitment to a partnership, and Bill had Saleh's unequivocal commitment to finish the job.

In diplomacy, celebrations of successes are rare and short-lived. Bill's immediate concern was getting to Riyadh. His flight from Sanaa was leaving imminently. I did not relish another helicopter ride. Political officer Steve Walker was acting as control officer for the visit and seized the initiative. In Saleh's presence, as we were leaving, he raised Bill's flight problem. Saleh said he would see what he could do. We expected news that Yemenia Airways was delaying the flight's departure from Sanaa. Instead, we learned that a Yemenia Boeing 737 was being flown to Aden to take only Bill and his party to Riyadh. In the event it took somewhat longer than promised because Saleh ordered a whole lamb prepared as the in-flight meal. Bill arrived in Riyadh in time and in style.

Within a week, we had a second senior visitor, FBI director Bob Mueller. Uniquely among senior Washington policymakers, Mueller had developed firsthand knowledge of Yemen and its president, which proved to be both a blessing and a curse. Counterterrorism in Yemen resembled the old adage about politics: like sausage making, the process was unedifying.

The FBI's experience in Yemen had been problematic from the outset. Following the *Cole* attack, the FBI wanted to flood Aden with agents and repeat its success of Nairobi where a compliant Kenyan government had essentially given over the investigation to the FBI. Acutely sensitive to foreign domination and interference, the Yemenis were not about to follow the Nairobi example. Ambassador Bodine had fought doggedly to obtain FBI access and a modicum of cooperation, with significant success. The embassy and Mueller were constantly trying to enlarge that cooperation.

As with other U.S. agencies, the FBI's best tool to do so were the Arab American agents who spoke fluent Arabic and related almost as brothers to Yemeni counterparts.[14] The lead investigator combined encyclopedic knowledge of al Qaeda, which resulted from work on the East African and *Cole* cases, with a nearly unique ability to engage Yemeni counterparts. The only time that I saw Yemen's intelligence head, General Gamish, smile sincerely in meeting an American visitor was when the lead investigator returned after a prolonged absence.

Unfortunately, the FBI had very few agents of this caliber and background, and they were stretched by work from New York to Pakistan. Instead, the U.S. embassy in Sanaa found itself with a series of temporary duty staff members. Few knew Arabic. All found the Yemenis impossible to understand. I set as an early goal the assignment of a permanent legal attaché to Sanaa—ideally an Arabic speaker.[15]

Bob Mueller arrived in Aden four days after Bill Burns. Unlike Bill, he had no concerns with air schedules, as he commanded an FBI Gulfstream jet. His security deployed in the Aden airport as if in a battle zone. It was forever a puzzle to Yemeni security officials why their same security arrangements for an assistant secretary of state should be judged totally inadequate for an FBI director.

In Mueller's meetings, the Yemeni desire to proceed with the prosecution of the *Cole* detainees was made clear to him. Separately, I also pressed for the assignment of a permanent legal attaché.

Meanwhile, al Qaeda was also escalating its activity in Yemen. Abd al-Rahim al-Nashiri had been responsible for its operations in the Arabian Peninsula for several years.[16] Mastermind of the successful attack against the *Cole*, he was now plotting a sequel with Abu Ali. Working from outside Yemen, he recruited Walid al-Shaibah to lead the operation. The initial target: tankers calling at the Yemeni oil terminal at Ash Shihr, near Al Mukalla.[17] Al Qaeda had achieved a tactical success in striking the USS *Cole*. Now it was aiming at Yemen's economic jugular.[18]

Al-Nashiri and al-Shaibah recruited others to the plot, including Hasan al-Badawi and Naser Awadh, who were assigned to roles as suicide bombers. Omar Said Hassan Jarallah was another key operative. From the $40,000 allocated to finance the operation, on February 12 he purchased a boat and outboard motors from the Daoud Trading Company in Al Hudaydah and had them transported to Al Mukalla. About the same time, the plotters rented a villa in Al Mukalla. From his base in Shabwah, Abu Ali provided the explosives.

Abu Ali was also directing a plot aimed at intimidating the Yemeni intelligence and security forces by striking at locations in Sanaa. For these actions, he recruited Fawaz al-Rabi'a, Abu Bakr al-Rabi'a, and Hizam Majali.[19] With C-3 and TNT obtained in Raydah, Fawaz fashioned bombs that his brother Abu Bakr placed at various locations around Sanaa. The first exploded at 6:30 a.m. on March 16. Its target: the Civil Aviation and Meteorological Authority building in central Sanaa. It caused significant material damage but no casualties. On March 18 the al Qaeda group then targeted the home of the PSO's head of counterterrorism branch, Brig. Gen. Mohammad al-Surmi. Subsequently, they placed bombs near the homes of Brig. Gen. Mohammad al-Hamdani and Maj. Gen. Ali Monsour Rashid, who was General Gamish's deputy in the PSO. Its headquarters in the Al Hadda district were struck on April 4. While creating a dramatic political effect, the bombs caused no serious casualties and relatively little material damage.

On April 10 the "Sympathizers with Al Qaeda" issued its public claim of responsibility for the bombing campaign. The statement castigated Saleh's government for imprisoning mujahideen and demanded the release of 173 prisoners, described as al Qaeda members, from PSO custody. Specifically mentioned was the father of Fawaz al-Rabi'a and Ahmed al-Hadda, an old but active mujahid who had been imprisoned in connection with the takedown of his house—the al Qaeda "logistic center" in Sanaa. The group's statement warned, "We swear to Allah, that if the cases of the prisoners are not resolved, the wheel of war will be steered toward senior officers and officials within thirty days . . . and then shift to political figures."[20]

Saleh and his government held firm. The bombing campaign tapered off and ended with an attack on the Communications Institute in the Sofan district of Sanna on May 9. The plot continued in Al Mukalla, however, and soon al Qaeda would prepare another campaign for Sanaa—this one targeted at Yemen's international supporters.

Given al Qaeda's escalation, U.S. moral and material support for Saleh's counterterrorism campaign took on some urgency. I was working with Interior Minister al-Alimi to implement several provisions of the memorandum, which had never been formally agreed on. My hope was our actions would prove better than our words. One pressing need was a system by which the Yemenis could control their borders, including airports and seaports. From the East Africa, *Cole*, and 9/11 investigations, we knew al Qaeda used Yemen as a transit point for travels to the Arabian Peninsula, East Africa, and East Asia. We calculated that screening against a reliable database would impede such travel. We also wanted to help the Yemenis deny entry to suspicious individuals and catch suspects trying to flee Yemen in the event of a terrorist act such as the attack on the *Cole*. Given Yemen's long land borders and coastline, any system would be imperfect, but 9/11 and other investigations showed that al Qaeda routinely did use legal points of entry.

Fortunately, I had helped initiate TIP while deputy director of S/CT. This program provided computers and related hardware and the PISCES software system to select countries.[21] While we accorded Pakistan top priority given its proximity to al Qaeda's base in Afghanistan, I had little trouble convincing the interior minister and S/CT that Yemen should be next. By mid-February, we were able to sign a brief memorandum of intent that covered a multiphased program including Yemen's international airports, Aden Port, and land crossings.

I had also inherited a commitment from my predecessor, endorsed by General Franks, to help Yemen develop its coast guard. The *Cole* incident evidenced the woeful inadequacy of Yemeni security forces in protecting Aden Port, one of Yemen's most important economic assets. Also vulnerable were Yemen's oil infrastructure and its rich fisheries, which were being plundered by foreign fishing fleets. While Yemen had a navy, at least on paper, my predecessor had correctly decided that the U.S. effort should be directed at a coast guard under the interior minister. President Saleh agreed and issued a decree establishing the institution. For an initial core fleet, the United States was to provide six or seven of its excess coast guard boats.

Unfortunately, the Yemeni Coast Guard project was becalmed and a symbol of pledges unfulfilled. CENTCOM viewed Yemen as a combat zone and refused to approve deployments of a U.S. Coast Guard officer to plan the force. I found Coast Guard commandant Adm. James M. Loy sympathetic[22]; the CENTCOM hierarchy less so. I explained my problem to al-Alimi, who volunteered protection around the clock. The U.S. Coast Guard officer would even have an office in one of the most secure locations in the country. Tampa relented, and Loy sent me Jim Willis, one of the U.S. Coast Guard's best.[23] Accompanied by Colonel Tewfiq, Willis traveled along the length of Yemen's coast—1,500 miles—and in April presented the Yemeni Coast Guard plan, which al-Alimi and I agreed to implement.

As the TIP and coast guard initiatives were progressing, I returned to Washington in late February for consultations. In addition to State, CIA, and FBI, all of which had

had senior visitors to Yemen, I called on General Downing in the NSC and on the Office of the Vice President, also located in the Eisenhower Executive Office Building next to the West Wing. The latter staff had a proposal: Vice President Dick Cheney envisioned a Middle East trip, largely to build support for our Iraq policy, and might stop by Sanaa if arrangements were suitable. I was delighted with the prospect. George H. W. Bush, the president's father, had been the senior-most U.S. official ever to visit Yemen and had done so as vice president. A Cheney visit would signal to Saleh an almost unprecedented level of attention. There was one snag. As with the FBI, the Office of the Vice President saw Yemen as a war zone. They preferred the meeting take place in a remote location, perhaps a military airport on the Omani border. If not that, then the most exposure they could envision was a brief stop at Sanaa's international airport. In Washington, I also had a brief photo op with President Bush during which I was able to give him a quick update on counterterrorism in Yemen. He was encouraging, and on that basis I promised a "message" to President Saleh.

I returned to Yemen in early March and asked to see the president in order to report on my Washington trip. Saleh was in Al Mukalla—ironically where al Qaeda was preparing its next attack—and also touring Ma'rib, Shabwah, and Al Jawf, which was most welcome presidential attention to the deprived areas. He asked me not to wait for his return to Sanaa but to see him there. I took with me Tom Hastings, a former Marine with whom I had worked in S/CT and who had been assigned temporarily to the U.S. embassy in Sanaa to help coordinate our counterterrorism effort. Tom and subsequent colleagues from S/CT contributed greatly to our understaffed country team.[24]

Saleh wanted to talk about increasing U.S. assistance to Ma'rib. His particular proposal entailed aid to both the military and civilian hospitals there. The military one was functioning and where the Yemeni casualties from the December 18 operation were treated. The new civilian hospital was only a shell with massive equipment and staffing needs. Saleh was also focused on the Yemeni Coast Guard: "Where are the boats?" He proposed to channel the cream of Yemen's military academy graduates to the new service. He also noted the training of the Yemeni Special Operations Forces (YSOF), commanded by his son Ahmed, which had gotten under way.[25] I pointed out that problems with clearing equipment, especially at Sanaa's airport, impeded this undertaking. I also informed him that Vice President Cheney would be in the Middle East and would like to stop in Yemen. Noting the security concerns of Cheney's staff, I relayed the proposal for a meeting at Sanaa International Airport. Saleh was predictably displeased: the United States was saying, in effect, that he did not even control his capital. Our security concerns appeared to reflect a lack of trust, especially since the first bomb of the Sympathizers with Al Qaeda group had not yet exploded. The mercurial president was in a good mood overall, however. President Bush's message was well received, and Saleh was persuaded to agree to an airport stop on March 14. I had used a considerable amount of political capital—progress on special forces's training and the coast guard—but with a significant political dividend in view.

Meanwhile, on the six-month anniversary of the 9/11 attacks, President Bush spoke on the South Lawn, updating the American people on the war on terror. Afghanistan was naturally the centerpiece, but the president also cited three other significant fronts—the Philippines, Georgia, and Yemen:

> Now that the Taliban are gone and al Qaeda has lost its home base for terrorism, we have entered the second stage of the war on terror—a sustained campaign to deny sanctuary to terrorists who would threaten our citizens from anywhere in the world. . . . In Yemen, we are working to avert the possibility of another Afghanistan. Many al Qaeda recruits come from near the Yemen-Saudi Arabian border, and al Qaeda may try to reconstitute itself in remote corners of that region. President Saleh has assured me that he is committed to confronting this danger. We will help Yemeni forces with both training and equipment and to prevent that land from becoming a haven for terrorists.[26]

Meanwhile, in Sanaa we were struggling with arrangements for the vice president's visit. The Secret Service advance party was naturally concerned with security. In this case, the operation was simplicity itself. The plane would land at the airport, and he would walk fifty paces to a presidential VIP lounge for his meetings. The visit was to be kept secret until it occurred. The Yemeni presidential office, however, could not resist: the news leaked, to the consternation of Washington. U.S. security demands escalated, and we asked urgently for meetings with the Ministry of Defense. The Yemenis stalled. Finally, the interior minister took the meeting. The reason for the delay was then apparent: he had been engaged in planning an extensive security operation that entailed stationing Yemeni security personnel on virtually every block of Sanaa's northern part. The Secret Service reluctantly agreed with the security arrangements, and the vice president arrived not in *Air Force Two* but in a C-17, no doubt equipped for missile threats and flown acrobatically in a corkscrew landing.

While immediate results of the visit were slim, it did engage the vice president and his staff in Yemen. They had seen at least the prospect of a partnership. While totally unsentimental, the Office of the Vice President on balance opted for Yemen as "partner, not target" in the Washington debate. Vice President Cheney himself would be willing to pick up the phone and lobby Saleh if need be.

The Yemeni-U.S. relationship was evolving much too positively to persist. I had long ago learned that in the Middle East things are rarely as good as they may seem and rarely as bad. Middle East politics exact a rough balance. In Yemen the correction would come from an unlikely direction: support flights and diplomatic pouches.

Saleh requested and we agreed that the YSOF should receive priority in our counterterrorism training. The Jordanians had been training the YSOF at their base on the outskirts of Sanaa. The YSOF had developed an impressive PowerPoint presentation on their organization as well as a slick demonstration that included intercepting a fleeing vehicle. Part of their canned demonstration included bringing guests into a pitch-black room in which a small YSOF unit then stormed with guns blazing to eliminate theoretical terrorists. Given shaky Yemeni fire discipline, one such episode was my limit in showing interest in their capability.

CENTCOM and other agency trainers picked up from the Jordanians, who very usefully agreed to stay on as interpreters.[27] U.S. Army Special Forces troops and U.S. Marines did much of the training. From the beginning, the relationship was tense. CENTCOM support flights arrived at Sanaa's military airport, which was actually one side of the international airport. Many parts of the Yemeni bureaucracy controlled arrangements and clearance procedures: the Yemeni military, civil aviation, and, most importantly, the PSO. The "target versus partner" issue reared its head in the guise of Yemeni insistence on inspecting and accounting for all equipment and arms entering their country. American trainers resented such inspections. On one occasion, Yemeni security forces and American trainers actually drew weapons on each other.

In Al Mukalla I had raised the issue with Saleh to try to head off such confrontations. While I received general assurances, the problems persisted. Similar tensions occurred in the special forces camp, especially when the American trainers entered or exited. The Yemenis wanted to know what equipment and weapons were being brought in and, more importantly, taken out.

Yemeni sensitivities became more and more acute. As part of our counterterrorism effort, the embassy was flying in a great deal of equipment to support our burgeoning temporary staff and activities. Much was mundane, including desks, computers, and building supplies. Normally, all material destined for the embassy's controlled access area was shipped in diplomatic pouches, long inviolable by virtue of the Vienna Convention governing diplomatic relations. Diplomatic pouches were a misnomer, however. In practice, most items were consolidated on large pallets, wrapped in burlap, and labeled "diplomatic pouch." The practice worked smoothly all over the world, but not in Sanaa.

The Yemenis had lodged an exception to the relevant part of the Vienna Convention, narrowly construing the concept of diplomatic pouch. For them, it meant the orange canvas bags more traditionally used, the largest of which might include a couple of computer monitors. Each support flight became a nightmare and occasioned confrontation. Even more galling to the embassy was the Yemeni practice of facilitating entry for any equipment or weapons we brought in that was destined for their use yet denying the embassy its equipment.

Initially, the exact "villain" remained obscure. Gradually, we found the Yemeni military slightly more helpful, but the PSO remained adamant. We tried confrontation. A support flight with equipment for both the Yemenis and the embassy arrived, and the pouches were unloaded. We refused inspections; the Yemenis refused to allow them off the airport's tarmac. We moved them to covered shelters on a corner of the airfield and arranged for cleared American troops to watch over them. Because we needed the military personnel to watch pouches, training was suspended. I protested at the Foreign Ministry, whose officials voiced sympathy but refused to concede Yemen's narrow interpretation of its responsibilities.

Finally, I had recourse to Abdulkarim al-Iryani, who, alone among Yemenis, would tell Saleh hard, uncomfortable truths. Al-Iryani informed me that the problem was not new. In constructing the embassy in the late 1980s, the Yemenis had also strictly insisted on inspecting the materials imported for its construction. Then an arrangement was agreed whereby the inspections occurred at the embassy in the presence of both Yemeni and American officials. He proposed a similar arrangement to resolve the current issue.

I saw merit in the approach, but some of my non-State staff remained inflexible. When we pointed out that much of the equipment was not sensitive and could be inspected by the Yemenis, so long as an American was on hand to prevent tampering, the response was that "not even a box of tissues" would be presented for Yemeni inspection. The State Department office charged with pouches also took a tough line, lest an important principle be compromised. However, it defined a category of "diplomatic cargo" that could be inspected but only under American watch. Meanwhile, CENT-COM, which needed to dramatically upscale its communications, had successfully passed even very sensitive equipment through Yemeni inspectors, who generally made comments to indicate their knowledge of the electronics and inventoried scrupulously in order to prove to their superiors they had performed their job. Nothing was compromised. Nothing was blocked.

Finally, I had recourse to President Saleh himself. I wrapped the issue in the most positive packaging I could: U.S.-Yemeni cooperation with the special forces, coast guard, and TIP. I explained Washington's sensitivities and even wove in a Yemeni fable. According to legend, the great dam of Ma'rib had been destroyed in antiquity because a rat gnawed away its foundation. The diplomatic pouch issue was similarly gnawing at the partnership Saleh had built with President Bush and Vice President Cheney. He was unimpressed and adamant. The embassy was not alone in its efforts. The NEA bureau of the State Department also raised the issue with Amb. Abdulwahab al-Hajri but to no avail.

The visit of General Franks in late June provided some much-needed "balm" on our sore relations. As usual, Saleh enjoyed Franks's direct, homespun manner, and the area for cooperation increased with Saleh's agreement to assign Yemeni liaison officers at CENTCOM headquarters in Tampa.

Unfortunately, the confrontations over diplomatic pouches had only worsened. On the Yemeni side, the PSO, with the president's backing, took increasingly restrictive positions, insisting at one stage to X-ray even the orange bags they conceded were proper diplomatic pouches. On our side, non-State staff had taken an equally hard-line position, although in private conversations some admitted that most of the equipment could be brought in as diplomatic cargo under U.S. control but subject to Yemeni inspection. I was still attempting to bridge the gap. Foreign Minister Qirby, his vice minister Abdullah al-Saidi, and Presidential Adviser al-Iryani had all tried to be helpful.

The Yemenis were paying a price for their hard line. For some time, we had linked delivery of weapons and equipment for their special forces to delivery of equipment for the embassy's activities. We had evolved to a classic lose-lose situation.

CHAPTER FIVE

NO SECURITY WITHOUT DEVELOPMENT

Before arriving in Yemen, I had worked on counterterrorism for two years in Washington and spent more than fifteen years in the Middle East. In that time, I had seen an ambiguous relationship between poverty and terrorism. One prevalent proposition was that terrorism represents a more or less inevitable reaction to material deprivation: desperate people take desperate measures. I had served in the Palestinian territories and knew the difficult living conditions of Palestinian refugees there and in Lebanon. I had also served seven years in Egypt during the crescendos of terrorism in the early '80s and mid-1990s and knew the grinding poverty there. The poverty-terrorism nexus seemed superficially credible.

Upon reflection, however, I thought it generally wrong and, as commonly stated, misleading. While some terrorists express solidarity with the poverty-stricken masses, individually they did not necessarily spring from deprived backgrounds. Osama bin Laden himself was a multimillionaire. His deputy, Ayman al-Zawahiri, was a doctor. The leadership of al Qaeda was often well educated and well employed. The 9/11 hijackers for the most part were Saudis who enjoyed many advantages of that relatively well-off society. Terrorists from the IRA, Baader-Meinhoff gang, Aum Shinrikyo, and other groups were not spawned from poverty. Conversely, the least developed countries of Africa did not necessarily produce terrorists. Moreover, a diagnosis that poverty was the root of terrorism suggested that terrorism could not be eliminated unless poverty were eliminated, a daunting prospect with profound resource implications.

Terrorists, however, do need operating space, which could be in the heart of cities or, significantly for al Qaeda, in remote areas where they enjoy the protection of local governments or tribes. In the initial brief for Colin Powell, the CSG had focused on al Qaeda's camps in Afghanistan. They were producing tens of thousands of trained terrorists.[1] They had to be shut down before we could hope to gain the initiative in the struggle against al Qaeda. Denying such safe havens and holding hosts responsible for terrorists on their soil were two fundamental lessons learned from 9/11.

Yemen, of course, was very different from Afghanistan. Its government was a responsible international actor whereas the Taliban had been a rogue regime designated by the United States and placed under sanctions by the UN Security Council as a sponsor of terrorism. While troubling connections did exist in Yemen between some government officials and mujahideen, stemming from the jihad in Afghanistan against the Soviet Union and Yemen's own civil war, the official policy rejected terrorism. Al Qaeda's real potential for safe haven resided in the remote tribal areas. The government's attempt on December 18, 2001, to apprehend terrorists affiliated with al Qaeda in Ma'rib and Shabwah had demonstrated the difficulties and risks of operating in a tribal environment hostile to government activity. As I saw it, the challenge in Yemen was to help its government extend control throughout the country, especially in remote locations, and convince the tribes that their interests lay with the government and not with al Qaeda.

President Saleh had pointed the way in a late-night phone call to me following his meeting with political and tribal leaders. The deprived areas required particular attention; could the United States help?[2]

Saleh had misconstrued my attempt to conceptualize an approach to the problem—Plan Ma'rib—because it highlighted the role of bad governance in the vicious circle of insecurity and underdevelopment. As with the aborted counterterrorism memorandum, I decided to implement the concept practically without seeking formal agreement. The objective, to strengthen government control, should have become clear both by how we went about our activities in full cooperation with Yemeni government authorities and in the result.

Ahmed Sufan, the deputy prime minister and minister of international cooperation, would prove to be a fine partner. Extremely voluble, Sufan was adept at absorbing the latest development trend, such as Millennium Goals or Poverty Reduction, and at producing the Yemeni documents required for increased development aid.[3] My "no development without security, no security without development" mantra was odd though. Normally development bureaucrats and experts share a humanitarian culture, while counterterrorism officials and experts share a security culture. As with oil and vinegar, they need to be shaken vigorously before they mix.

Sufan usefully suggested that we spend a day together touring U.S.-supported projects in 'Amran in late October 2001. I found him a delightful traveling companion with a nearly unique variety of expertise. By profession a businessman, he needed no convincing of the essential role of the private sector in sustainable development, and he maintained important relations with Yemen's powerful business clans who were extremely skeptical of the country's government. Sufan was also a politician; he was in fact the only government minister to be elected to the parliament in 2003. As such, he knew firsthand the dynamics of government projects and popular support. And finally as a manager, he had built a competent staff, particularly Nabil Shaiban and Hisham Sharabi, with whom we could function effectively. The memorandum experience with the presidency had been painful and fruitless. With Sufan's ministry, such memoranda flowed from common objectives with relatively little effort.

Two other institutions proved to be trumps in the development game. The Social Fund, led by Minister of Labor Abdulkarim al-Arhabi,[4] and the Public Works Project, headed by Abdullah Sa'id, were unusually efficient institutions. With encouragement from the World Bank and the International Monetary Fund, they had been created outside the normal Yemeni bureaucracy to construct a social safety net and enable economic reforms. They paid staff well, and consequently their staffs included the best and brightest in Yemen.[5] Their female development specialists were particularly impressive. Al-Arhabi managed the Social Fund to achieve results with low administrative costs. His organization won international renown as a best practice.[6]

The embassy unfortunately could not begin to match Yemen's talent. Because of the country's vote in the UN Security Council against Desert Storm in 1990, our USAID mission had been dismantled and aid-funding almost eliminated. The authorized departure policy triggered by security concerns meant we had no economic section. In my mind, essential tools in the counterterrorism effort were lacking. But, by and large, Washington did not view development as an essential activity. Staffing could wait.

Ever resourceful, the embassy found expertise to fill the gap. Our Foreign Service nationals—Shaif al-Hamdany, Ahmed Attieg, and Fawzia Yousef—stepped into the American roles competently. Mac McAteer, a retired Foreign Service officer who had served previously in Yemen, agreed to come on temporary duty and brought with him experience and good humor.[7] Even our embassy doctor, who had public health expertise, would take on extra work with the Ministry of Health to further development. Later, when Colin Powell's Diplomatic Readiness Initiative began to bring a wealth of entry-level officers into the Foreign Service and to Sanaa, we recruited Gareth Harries, the spouse of one of our consular officers, who had development expertise and a gift for teamwork.

Although our USAID program had been dismantled, my predecessors, especially Ambassador Bodine, had creatively exploited the U.S. Department of Agriculture's (USDA's) 416b program. Largely owing to the American farm lobby, excess wheat, dried milk, and other commodities were shipped to Yemen and sold, and the Yemeni currency thus generated was used for development. Sufan's staff managed the program in Yemen, and Ellen Levinson, an astute lobbyist with long Yemeni experience, adeptly promoted its interests with USDA. Prior to my arrival, 416b funds had financed useful projects throughout Yemen, such as schools, agricultural roads, orphanages, and municipal gardens.

I thought this excellent program could be improved in two ways. First, there was little recognition for the U.S. taxpayer of the good work being accomplished. The signs that identified projects emphasized their executor, the Social Fund or the Public Works Project, and not the funder. Hence, the Yemenis viewed the United States as a nonplayer in development. The embassy had no public diplomacy staff, again because under authorized departure such work was deemed nonessential. And again, we improvised. Sanaa's great tower houses featured half-moon shaped windows with elaborate floral designs called *qamariyas*.[8] Although initially characteristic of northern houses, this architectural feature had spread throughout Yemen. We designed our own version, which incorporated both an American and Yemeni flag, and set about to "brand" our development efforts accordingly on project sites and in our literature.[9]

My second concern was the diffusion of projects. A school here and an orphanage there meant little developmental or political impact. If we concentrated our limited resources in the deprived areas, we could then tilt the security balance in favor of the government and also pioneer development so that other international donors could feel safe to expand their activities to these remote areas. A virtuous circle of security and development would thereby be created. For public diplomacy as well, projects needed prominence to register in public opinion. Diffuse and undefined efforts lacked visibility.[10]

I pitched my Plan Ma'rib concept to the international donors at an informal coordinating dinner, graciously hosted by Japanese ambassador Oki. The Germans welcomed more attention to Ma'rib since they had an ambitious archaeological project there. The Dutch had had a relatively ambitious assistance program but were confronting budget cuts and sought possible donors for some well-conceived but unfunded projects.

Meanwhile, Saleh seemed to send a signal by replacing Ma'rib's corrupt governor. To me, it appeared as if he were addressing the "good governance" arc of the vicious circle. I determined to respond tangibly and asked my staff to plan a trip to Yemen's "wild, wild east."

No ambassador moved outside Sanaa without permission from the Yemeni government.[11] The embassy sent a diplomatic note that detailed the trip's purpose, itinerary, and proposed meetings, and received formal permission to proceed. The embassy security officer then coordinated security with the Ministry of Interior, which usually consisted of two dishkas (pick-up trucks with a heavy machine gun mounted in the bed and about ten security troops) to lead and follow the convoy. Often additional arrangements were made with the prominent sheikhs of the region, in this case with Sheikh Rabish, whose town of Madghil sat just off the main road two-thirds of the distance to Ma'rib. Substantively, the embassy development team coordinated with the Social Fund and the Public Works Project.[12]

We launched in early morning of February 20, skirting the airport and traveling quickly through Sanaa's hinterland graced with grapevines but also littered by the multicolored plastic bags in which a day's chew of khat was sold.[13] Soon we could see on our right Noah's Ark, a dramatic rock formation. A path, supposedly marked by the prophet himself, led halfway up to the top before the climber penetrated a natural doorway and then scaled a perilous route the rest of the way.[14] Farther down the road, our convoy passed through a natural pass on which Sanaa's military had emplaced a tank with its turret pointing eastward as a caution to any force of tribesmen approaching the capital.

In about two hours, we reached Ma'rib and met briefly with the deputy governor. He welcomed us profusely, provided refreshments, and then proposed tourism. His ideas focused on Ma'rib's archaeological treasures. Our priorities differed. We were there not to sightsee, but to assess our potential role in Ma'rib's development. Guided by the Social Fund and the Public Works Project experts, we visited a dilapidated school first, then toured the Sun Temple (or Bar'an Temple) restored by German archaeologists, and drove by the even larger archaeological project of the American Foundation for the Study of Man to excavate the Moon Temple (or Mahram Bilqis).[15]

We also saw the small military hospital where the Yemeni casualties of the December 18 operations had been treated. It was the district's only functioning hospital and treated civilians as well. Finally, the local officials took us to the vast, new civilian hospital. It was an ambitious project but risked being Ma'rib's white elephant. Ma'rib was rich in oil, and a small part of those revenues had gone to construct the building. There was unfortunately no money for equipment or for training a staff. As such, the Ma'rib hospital appeared a potential monument to bad governance and neglect of its region's basic needs.

On the way back, we saw one more proposed project. We stopped in Madghil where Sheikh Rabish had some forty rugged tribesmen, each armed with a jambiyya and a Kalashnikov, arrayed in a crescent for our welcome. I moved along the half-moon shaking hands and greeting each: *Salaam alikum* (Peace be with you), *Masa' al khir* (Good afternoon), *Kif halkum* (How are you?), *Sharafna* (We are honored). We were then taken to a pathetic, ill-equipped building, which served as the town clinic. As Sheikh Abdullah al-Ahmar had advised me, health care ranked high on the tribe's list. The Social Fund was proposing a new clinic and living accommodations for permanent staff, both of which I told Sheikh Rabish we would fund. We returned to Sanaa.

The Madghil clinic turned out to cost only $250,000, and past 416b revenues were more than adequate. Our more ambitious development plans, however, were in serious jeopardy. The incoming Bush administration had agreed that the off-budget 416b program should be phased out and all development assistance put on budget. It was perfectly rational but also a potential disaster for our objective of promoting counterterrorism in Yemen.

President Bush had stated America's counterterrorism strategy in his remarks on the six-month anniversary of 9/11. In Afghanistan, where we had fought a war, that strategy specifically included development, namely "clearing mine fields, rebuilding roads and improving health care."[16] In Yemen, which featured prominently in the president's remarks, our commitment was focused solely on security. Earlier, in the immediate aftermath of 9/11, he had spoken of using all instruments of power,[17] but on the frontlines in Yemen there appeared to be a gap between words and deeds.

On relatively frequent consultations in Washington, I did my best to close the gap. At the annual meeting of Middle East ambassadors in February, which gave Secretary Powell's "battalion commanders" access to State's policymakers, I pressed the point. In return, I received sympathy and general commitments to include requests for development assistance in the post-9/11 supplemental request being prepared for Congress. My initial proposal for Plan Ma'rib had included a figure of $200 million. Of the $27.1 billion supplemental, Yemen's share was pegged at just $25 million of which $20 million was for military support and only $5 million for economic development.[18]

The overall problem was not lack of resources. The problem was "old think" in State and particularly its NEA bureau. State proposed that the vast majority of resources continue to go to three countries: Israel, Egypt, and Jordan. In the pre-9/11 world, both the administration and Congress had given priority to supporting the Arab-Israeli peace process. In NEA's bureaucratic mind-set, 9/11 had not significantly altered that calculus.[19]

The embassy was left to scrounge resources from various pots of money. Most important was the 416b pipeline. Sales from excess agricultural commodities would provide $63 million in fiscal years 2001 and 2002. In contrast, Economic Support Funds—the traditional source for economic assistance—totaled only $12 million for those years. Even that $12 million was going nowhere, since USAID was administering it from USAID Cairo, which was preoccupied by Egypt's own program and burgeoning new responsibilities in Afghanistan.

Ambassador Bodine had again proved enterprising in her pursuit of funds for mine clearance in Yemen. Here, too, Yemen's program was another international best practice. I had initially underestimated the program's significance, but my deputy Brad Hanson and an early trip to Aden changed my mind. When I witnessed the demining activity and the enthusiastic praise America received for its pioneering support, I became a convert.[20]

Assistant Secretary Bill Burns provided another potentially important funding source in MEPI. Long before the White House identified as a primary U.S. goal promoting democracy in the Middle East,[21] Bill had focused on developing a "positive agenda" for the United States to use in its relations with the Arab world. It concentrated on advocating indigenous reform efforts in four areas, or "pillars": education, economic development, good governance, and women's rights. It drew from the Arabs' own analysis of their societies' problems as articulated in the UN Human Development Report.[22] Management of the program was located in the NEA bureau, marginalizing the bureaucratically muscle-bound USAID. Finally, Deputy Assistant Secretary Liz Cheney was to be its CEO.

From the outset, the U.S. embassy in Sanaa enjoyed an advantage in competing for MEPI resources despite its lack of staff. For the U.S. embassy in Cairo or in Amman, MEPI moneys were relatively insignificant in comparison with existing aid programs. In places such as Riyadh and other Gulf capitals, government resources were generally adequate, and embassy staffs were not oriented to development work. We were "hungry," and we found among Yemeni nongovernmental organizations many reformers willing to engage on MEPI terms. From first-year resources (FY 2002) of $29 million, the U.S. embassy in Sanaa obtained more than any other single country: $3.8 million.

In a sense, America's most remarkable contribution to Yemen's economy was Hunt Oil Company's pioneering work in discovering oil near Ma'rib in 1984 and its subsequent development of hydrocarbon resources.[23] In preparing for my duty, I traveled to Houston and met the oil company's chairman, Ray Hunt, and some of his key associates. I found Ray modest, considerate, and appealing. I found the entire Hunt team extraordinarily knowledgeable about Yemen's geology, geography, and politics. In Abdulkarim Abu Hamad, Ray had tapped an extremely competent and charming Arab American to manage Hunt's activities and watch over Hunt's interests in Yemen.[24] Those interests stretched from its production facility just east of Ma'rib, across Yemen in the form of its pipeline, to the *Saafir*, a venerable supertanker in the Red Sea where Yemen's oil was stored and loaded onto transport tankers. To facilitate travel across this distance, Hunt operated a Bell/Agusta helicopter out of Sanaa's airport. Abdulkarim and I had twice used this helicopter: on my initial tour of the *Saafir* in February and a later tour of Hunt's processing unit near Ma'rib. Al Qaeda had taken note.

In mid-October, the international donors to Yemen gathered under World Bank auspices in Paris. The venue did not appeal to me. It seemed odd for government and international officials to meet in the luxurious surroundings of a European capital to discuss poverty in Yemen. However, the Yemenis, particularly Ahmed Sufan, took a dim view of travel to the World Bank headquarters in Washington given the stringent and often embarrassing security checks imposed after 9/11 on foreigners, particularly Yemenis, upon entry to the United States. For their part, the Europeans and other donors did not relish travel to Sanaa, a "war zone" in the war on terror.

I had an additional problem with Paris. General Franks was scheduled to visit Sanaa on October 17, and I could attend only the first day of the two-day meeting. Bill Burns agreed to represent the United States on day two. In my opening statement, I stressed the connections between development and security. I defended expenditures on counterterrorism (although not a recently announced extravagant purchase of MiG-29 fighters[25]) as cost effective and necessary to create an environment in which development efforts could go forward. I pushed for more effort in the deprived areas. Then I left. Bill's participation won praise as he was one of the most senior government representatives in attendance. The Yemenis appreciated his travel from Washington and his encouraging words on U.S. assistance.

After some creative accounting, the World Bank organizers announced that international donors had pledged $2.3 billion to help Yemen.[26] Little of it was new; it stretched over several years. I understood the Yemeni perception that the international community was lagging in its support. The United States needed to lead, I felt, especially in the critical areas of Ma'rib, Al Jawf, and Shabwah. I asked my staff to prepare a second trip to Ma'rib. We scheduled it for November 3 and 4.

CHAPTER SIX

INTO THE RED ZONE

As 2002 progressed, so did al Qaeda's plotting in Yemen. The bombing campaign by the Sympathizers with Al Qaeda group in Sanaa had not had its intended effect. The prisoners of interest to al Qaeda were not released. The Yemeni government persisted in its counterterrorism cooperation with the United States. Publicly, Saleh and his government identified themselves as part of the international coalition against al Qaeda, whose vision of Yemen as an alternate to Afghanistan was being frustrated. From outside Yemen, Abd al-Rahim al-Nashiri, al Qaeda's operations chief in the Arabian Peninsula, escalated operations.

The plot against Yemen's oil infrastructure continued. As proposed by al-Nashiri and Abu Ali, Walid al-Shaibah and his group pursued its preparations in Al Mukalla. The attack boat purchased in Al Hudaydah had been moved in place. Omar Jarallah, Fawzi al-Hababi, and Mohammed al-Amari undertook to rig the boat with explosives. The suicide bombers, Hasan al-Badawi and Naser Awadh, had accepted their roles. As in Aden in 2000, their activity passed unnoticed by the Yemeni security authorities and unreported by the local Yemenis who witnessed it. We perceived ongoing al Qaeda activity, but did not focus on Al Mukalla, rather on Al Hudaydah and Aden. As we assessed likely targets, the *Saafir*, Yemen's supertanker storage terminal just north of Al Hudaydah, appeared most vulnerable and most likely.

Given al Qaeda's success in attacking the embassies in Nairobi and Dar es Salaam in 1998, we also assumed the embassy was a prime target. The EAC met regularly to assess threats and adopt countermeasures. Some of the countermeasures were permanent. Jim Stone, a local American contractor, had strung concertina wire procured as excess from the U.S. military along the top of the embassy perimeter wall.[1] He had also replaced the grillwork that constituted the perimeter barrier at the embassy front with a reinforced wall. This wall proved useful on March 15, 2002, when a young Yemeni man, angered by U.S. support for Israel in the midst of the second Palestinian Intifada, threw two hand grenades at the embassy. One made it over the wall, and the other bounced off it. Both exploded, causing little damage and no injuries. The embassy's local guard force and CSF personnel subdued the man.[2]

Our Marine security guards handled their routine responsibilities and the occasional crisis with the utmost professionalism. In other postings, Jerusalem and Cairo, I had dealt with incidents of young Marines running afoul of local customs, but the detachment in Sanaa was known throughout the battalion for exceptionally high standards.[3] The influx of U.S. military personnel—trainers and liaison officers—significantly boosted the embassy's human resources, and the regional security officer integrated this considerable talent into the internal defense plan. These specialists also willingly trained our Foreign Service officers and local staff to detect tampering with their vehicles and helped us assess our vulnerabilities to mortars, rockets, and even surface-to-air missiles. State's Bureau of Diplomatic Security also provided full support: chem/bio trainers and equipment, surveillance detection training, and VIP protection training. Our colleagues in Washington were undertaking extraordinary efforts to safeguard us.

In Interior Minister al-Alimi, we had a most reliable partner. Many American ambassadors elsewhere had to plead or even threaten to get enhanced protection. Al-Alimi responded willingly and often went beyond my requests, even once closing off to traffic the two lanes of the avenue bordering our front wall. Col. Yahya Saleh, commander of CSF, took a personal interest in our security as well. He was known to visit his troops late at night to assess their readiness and personally investigated incidents such as the grenade attack. No defense provides guarantees, but the embassy was a hard target.

And targets we were. In the wake of its failed campaign against Yemeni security forces, al-Nashiri and Abu Ali directed that al Qaeda's bombing campaign shift from Yemeni officials to diplomatic targets. The American, British, German, French, and, inexplicably, the Cuban embassies made their list.[4] The Walid al-Shaibah group, still undertaking the Al Mukalla plot, was merged with the Fawaz al-Rabi'a group, which had undertaken the earlier bombing campaign in Sanaa. Most of their activity focused on the American embassy.[5]

The plotters rented a house on Socotra Street in the Al Qadissiyya district of Sanaa and purchased two cars. At least four of the plotters—Fawzi al-Wajeeh, Fawzi al-Hababi, Abu Bakr al-Rabi'a, and Ibrahim Howaidi—cased the American embassy.[6] Given the embassy defenses, the plotters decided a rocket attack was most feasible. Abu Ali help the plotters procure rockets and explosives from the Talhi arms bazaar north of Sa'dah. They transported two rockets, 337 kilograms of TNT, and rocket-propelled grenades with launchers from Sa'dah to Sanaa in plastic cartons covered with pomegranates. Circuit boards and Casio watches were rigged as triggers.[7]

Meanwhile, Yemeni-U.S. counterterrorism cooperation continued to suffer from serious growing pains. In Washington pressure mounted to get results in Yemen, and there were semiserious suggestions to invade the country. To those of us who knew its rugged terrain and fiercely independent tribes, that course of action appeared extremely costly and fraught with risks. The discussions indicated that the "target versus partner" debate was far from resolved.

The FBI had also detected suspicious activity among an expatriate group of Yemenis in upstate New York. Individuals deemed to have terrorist links had stockpiled thermoses and night-vision devices. The bureau theorized that the thermoses could be rigged as bombs to threaten airplanes, and the night-vision devices could be used for other terrorist operations. The Immigration and Naturalization Service issued an order to subject all Yemenis to secondary inspections at ports of entry and departure.

They naturally resented being singled out from other nationalities. The minister of foreign affairs suggested less insidious explanations for Yemeni nationals' interest in thermoses and night-vision devices. The former were ubiquitous at Yemeni khat chews; the thermoses kept warm the sweet tea that countered the dehydrating effects of chewing khat. The latter were extremely handy for Yemeni farmers guarding khat groves from nighttime prowlers.[8] In the superheated security climate following 9/11, such explanations carried little weight. While noting less menacing explanations, we pressed for the FBI to conclude its investigation and establish the facts one way or another. Initially, political relief came from the opposite direction: Pakistanis and Saudis were subjected to similar treatment. The miserable Yemenis loved the company.

The escalating Palestinian Intifada created its own political headwind for our efforts in Yemen. The Arabic news channels and print media supplied a steady stream of graphic images that inflamed Yemeni sentiment and prompted the embassy grenade attack. The negative impact was palpable. Discussion of Yemeni-U.S. cooperation often took place literally with an Al Jazeera broadcast of suffering Palestinians in the background.[9] President Bush's promotion of a two-state solution in his June 24 speech as well as Secretary Powell's and Bill Burns's efforts to define the "road map" to that solution helped us significantly manage the issue's corrosive effects on counterterrorism cooperation.

By summer 2002 that cooperation was taking increasingly tangible form, but not without considerable friction. U.S. Special Forces soldiers and Marines were well along in training the YSOF. The Yemeni recruits provided excellent raw material. They were tough and motivated. According to my Special Forces advisers, their basic skills were surprisingly good. Their Jordanian trainers provided both interpreters and model soldiers. But two questions haunted the program. First, the YSOF's real mission proved elusive. In their command briefing, counterterrorism was emphasized. However, they had not deployed for the December 18 fiasco, and their deployments generally seemed more in keeping with a praetorian guard than a true special operations force. As in most Arab countries, regime protection appeared to be the priority. Second, they lacked noncommissioned officers. As in most of the Arab world, there was a gap between the officers, who were making a career of the military, and the recruits. Nevertheless, the first trainees graduated in July. Their impact in the struggle against al Qaeda remained a question mark as we helped the Yemenis develop plans and intelligence to test the YSOF's effectiveness.

An allied country, Britain, played a role in training the Yemenis as well.[10] We greatly respected their expertise and welcomed a partnership. With fewer resources and limited time, they agreed to focus on the Interior Ministry's CSF, led by Col. Yahya Saleh. When the British finished their initial training, their U.S. counterparts took over the mission. The British government eventually agreed to renew the effort, and we alternated in continuous CSF training thereafter. This related effort unfortunately included no equipping, but the United States stepped in to provide equipment equal to that supplied the YSOF.

Unfortunately, progress on the training grounds was not lubricating the support flights with their diplomatic pouches. Washington, including the vice president, had been helpful. I had had my own heart-to-heart with the president. All to little avail.

Each support flight became a drama. Material for Yemeni use was quickly approved. Material for embassy use and classified pouches were questioned and subject to delay. Radios, weapons, and blood for use should American trainers suffer an injury were held up and only reluctantly allowed in. These frictions not only hampered our local efforts, but they also began to impact Washington's assessment of Yemen's commitment to counterterrorism. I briefed Presidential Adviser al-Iryani and asked him to share my concern with President Saleh. Meanwhile, the foreign minister made a good faith effort to coordinate among the Yemeni players a compromise on diplomatic pouches.

In some ways, Americans and Yemenis were adopting mirror positions. Spooked by the thermoses and night-vision devices in upstate New York, U.S. authorities had imposed draconian measures on all Yemenis entering or leaving the United States. Of course, we understood these measures to be prudent precautions given our experience on September 11. The Yemenis, particularly the PSO, had reciprocal doubts about U.S. intentions and activities. Was equipment for the stated purpose of fostering the partnership or a more nefarious purpose? Was Yemen a partner or a target?

We, including Vice President Cheney, had exercised diplomatic leverage and practical leverage, such as holding up Yemeni equipment, but had not forced a solution. Some in the embassy and back in Washington wanted to escalate. A few embassy sections opted for all-out confrontation, convinced that Saleh would and could be compelled. Relations with some counterparts deteriorated dramatically. I thought it was the wrong tactic and the wrong issue. With Yemeni officials and with the Yemeni public, a confrontation over the country's control of entry and exit of material or people would be perceived as a confrontation over its sovereignty. Yemeni pride would be engaged; no practical price would be deemed too high.

Moreover, in critical ways, cooperation was progressing. Haltingly, we were developing realistic options for striking al Qaeda in Yemen. Admittedly, there were problems—often from Yemen but sometimes from the United States as well. Equipment went down, the weather impeded. Not surprisingly, Washington began to consider other approaches, seeking to apply the relative success in Afghanistan to a radically different situation in Yemen. The embassy and CENTCOM supported each other as voices of reason to temporarily restrain Washington's more bellicose players.

We were at a tipping point, and al Qaeda came to our assistance. On August 9 Walid al-Shaibah and Bashir al-Safari were preparing their rockets for the attack on the embassy, which was scheduled for Tuesday, August 13. One rocket misfired and impacted one of the terrorists in the chest. He died immediately. The other had his hand blown off and died while being taken to the hospital. Fawaz and Abu Bakr al-Rabi'a were in the next room. They escaped.

Saleh urgently summoned me the following day. It appeared to him that the plotters may have been targeting the president himself, and he welcomed assistance in investigating the plot. From the embassy, my counterterrorism team reached back for help. NCIS was first off the mark. They had resources in the area and knew Yemen well from the USS *Cole* investigation. Their representative on the Country Team had investigators on the ground within hours. Initially, the FBI hesitated. No Americans had been harmed, and at this stage it was not known that the terrorists' target was the American embassy. Within hours, however, the FBI also reached the decision to send specialists. Since NCIS and the FBI had worked hand in glove on the *Cole* investigation, I had no concerns with coordination.

Admiral Keating, my interlocutor at the Pentagon on 9/11 and now commander of the Fifth Fleet, arrived on a previously scheduled visit on August 12 and found his NCIS investigators at work. He graciously agreed to visit Aden as well, where he could see firsthand the Yemeni demining program, which his command was also supporting, and Aden Port. We met with the port authority and Yemeni officials. He agreed with me that the U.S. Navy's resumption of refueling was feasible.

In late August Saleh addressed the ruling party's congress and focused on terrorism. Previously, he had been characteristically erratic on the issue of al Qaeda, at times denying publicly that they had any presence in Yemen. Perhaps sobered by the Al Qadissiyya incident, he acknowledged that al Qaeda was present. He held al Qaeda accountable for attacks against the country's interests but offered them a chance to surrender. They would not be handed over to the Americans but rather subject to Yemeni justice and be considered innocent until proven guilty.[11] Yemeni efforts to convince Abu Ali to surrender continued but failed to produce a result.

On September 21, CSF took down a house in Rawdah, a northern suburb of Sanaa near the international airport. The operation had not been coordinated with the PSO, and the scene was confused. The target, Yahya al-Majali, had terrorist connections and fought to the death. A security force officer suffered a serious wound to his leg. Minister al-Alimi invited us to help process the scene and asked our assistance in treating his wounded man. We were well prepared to help with the crime scene.[12] Aiding the wounded proved problematic, however. U.S. agencies had been generous in providing medical treatment of Yemeni security personnel harmed in joint training. They were understandably cautious, however, about taking responsibility for those injured in unilateral Yemeni operations and declined to assist.

The Yemeni officer's condition quickly deteriorated as gangrene set in. The embassy physician, Curt Hofer, a former U.S. Army doctor well versed in combat injuries, reported that the leg needed to be amputated. The patient reluctantly agreed. Once again, I had recourse to our Jordanian friends. I knew that Amman's King Hussein Medical Center offered first-class treatment. I asked my Jordanian counterpart, Amb. Mohamed al-Khaldi, for help and also asked our embassy in Amman to weigh in. The Jordanians had been relatively generous in their counterterrorism assistance to the Yemenis and had not always been recognized for it. They shared our agencies' reluctance to take responsibility for the injured man. With only vague assurances, we found the means to transport the man to Amman, and the Jordanian government came through as both Mohamed and I had expected they would. The Yemeni's life had been saved.

The Ministry of Interior and particularly CSF demonstrated in Rawdah a willingness to put U.K.-U.S. training and equipment into the battle against terrorism. The will of the YSOF remained questionable, although its capability had clearly been enhanced by our efforts, and we witnessed an impressive exercise of that improved capability at the end of September.

Al Qaeda made the next move. The long-prepared Al Mukalla plot culminated in an attack on the French oil tanker M/V *Limburg* on October 6. One crewman, a Bulgarian, was lost overboard and died. Initial reports were sketchy and misleading. As with the *Cole*, there was initially a possibility that the explosion was an accident. With only photos of the damage, U.S. experts initially credited this explanation.

The embassy had now been through a number of such incidents. Our policy was simple. Withhold judgment and get professional investigators on the scene to collect the facts. Having learned its lessons well, the Yemeni government issued cautious public statements.

Foreign Minister al-Qirby asked for U.S. help in the investigation. Again, NCIS, followed by the FBI, was there within hours. Based on the material evidence and eyewitnesses, they and the Yemenis quickly agreed it was a terrorist act. The U.S. investigators then found conclusive evidence linking the M/V *Limburg* attack to known al Qaeda operatives.

Yemeni reaction, both official and popular, was immediate and outraged. Terrorists had struck at Yemen's economic jugular. Fortunately, damage to the tanker was limited. It had not yet loaded its cargo, so the resulting spill was also limited. Nevertheless, fishing beds were polluted. Insurance premiums for vessels using Yemeni ports skyrocketed.

Yemen did not lack high-level U.S. attention in the aftermath of the M/V *Limburg* attack. The State Department's counterterrorism coordinator, Frank Taylor, arrived on October 8 and was most welcome. In our initial briefing of then secretary-designate

Powell in December 2000, I had pressed him to make the appointment of State's counterterrorism coordinator a high priority. Having witnessed with admiration Mike Sheehan's galvanizing effect on our counterterrorism diplomacy, I had done my best to fill Mike's shoes when he departed in December 2000. Frank had more than adequately filled mine since July 2001. From his resources, he supplied the embassy every support possible: experts such as Tom Hastings, funding for TIP, Anti-terrorism Assistance, and his own strong voice of reason in Washington policy circles. Frank found President Saleh "feisty but friendly."

General Franks followed with a visit in mid-October. On October 28, Yemen was finally added to CENTCOM's coalition list in the global war on terror, thereby formally designating the country a partner, not a target.

Ever welcome, Bill Burns showed up in late October. Saleh praised his attendance and speech at the Paris meeting of the donors' coordinating group. As Saleh had not unreasonably decided that Yemen could benefit greatly from a free trade agreement, Bill was an ideal interlocutor on the subject since he had managed a success in Jordan as ambassador there.[13] Both Palestine and Iraq were very much on Saleh's mind. On Palestine, Bill briefed authoritatively on the continuing efforts of the Quartet (the United States, Russia, European Union [EU], and United Nations) to implement the road map to President Bush's proposed two-state solution. On Iraq, however, we shared little common ground. Saleh usefully made clear that agreement on neither Palestine nor Iraq was a condition for counterterrorism cooperation.

On Iraq, Saleh was nevertheless determined to do what he could to avert the looming U.S.-Iraqi confrontation. Yemen had paid dearly for its failure to support Operation Desert Storm in 1990, and Saleh did not want a repeat. Presidential Adviser al-Iryani was Saleh's designated envoy to advise Saddam Hussein that he had no alternative but to accept UN Security Council demands. After his visit to Baghdad at this time, al-Iryani provided me his impressions. He had found Saddam buoyed by his recent overwhelming election as president, which, al-Iryani observed sardonically, had been in true Arab fashion, with more than 99 percent of the vote. Saddam, al-Iryani also reported, was convinced that the United States was determined "to get" him. Iraq would cooperate for the sake of the international community and its friends, but Iraqi officials knew such cooperation would not save it from America's wrath. They offered Yemen 5 million barrels of oil for political consideration.[14] Yemen had been among Iraq's most stalwart supporters in the first Gulf War, but Baghdad now realized how far Sanaa had shifted since then. Tommy Franks's visit was the symbol of improved

U.S.-Yemeni relations, and Iraqi vice president Taha Ramadan was furious about it, according to al-Iryani.

As we entered November 2002, the embassy's counterterrorism team had cause for optimism. True, our intelligence continued to indicate clear and present threats, but cooperation with the Yemenis had improved significantly. Personnel changes had created a new consensus in the embassy to work around the pouch issues, and bilateral strains had eased.

Al Qaeda had also committed serious mistakes. Targeting the M/V *Limburg* and Yemen's oil lifeline had rallied the government and considerable parts of the population against it. Belatedly, the Yemeni government had come to realize that its public had a role to play in counterterrorism. Saleh's media adviser, Faris Sanibani, told us that the president had noted that an ordinary American citizen had been instrumental in the arrest of the snipers who had recently been stalking the Washington, D.C., area. If Americans could help their government confront the snipers, why couldn't Yemenis provide similar help against terrorists? The Yemeni media machine shifted into a higher gear, and ordinary citizens for the first time were enlisted in the cause.[15]

The misfire in Al Qadissiyya had also removed al Qaeda's most effective operator, Walid al-Shaibah, from the scene, exposed the al Qaeda operation against the American embassy, and alarmed Saleh. Abu Ali was still masterminding overall al Qaeda operations in Yemen, but he was on the run. In one embassy meeting, I expressed cautious optimism. I likened our situation to an American football team that had advanced the ball within the twenty-yard line: we were "in the red zone."

Al Qaeda quickly shifted its tactics. Its previous primary target, the American embassy, had proven too hard. Even if al-Shaibah had successfully modified his rockets, a standoff attack with them (that is, one allowing them to avoid defensive fire) would have probably produced relatively few casualties and little damage. Fawaz al-Rabi'a and Abu Bakr al-Rabi'a had themselves barely escaped from the scene of the August 9 misfire. Abu Ali now instructed them to focus on a softer target: the Hunt Oil Company's helicopter.

Hunt's helicopter was easier on several counts. First, it was not and could not be hardened to any great extent. More importantly, its operation was predictable. It flew on schedule either eastward to the Ma'rib production facility or westward to the *Saafir* supertanker storage facility off Al Hudaydah. Fawaz al-Rabi'a took the lead. Beyond planning the operation, he was responsible for firing the missile at the aircraft. An associate, Hizam Majali, would simultaneously shoot at the helicopter with a machine gun. Mohamed al-Dailami would drive the getaway car, and Abu Bakr al-Rabi'a would videotape the operation. The group, which also included 'Aref Majali, collected SAM-7s (Soviet-designed surface-to-air missiles), a machine gun, and four AK-47s for the assault.[16]

On November 3 at about 6:45 a.m., Ibrahim Howaidi was in position to monitor the helicopter's movement from a building at the airport. He informed the assault group as it took off in the direction of Ma'rib. Fawaz al-Rabi'a fired the missile but missed. Hizam Majali had better results. Two bullets hit the helicopter, one of which slightly injured two of the Hunt employees on board.[17] The helicopter returned safely to Sanaa International Airport within minutes.

One of the attackers, 'Aref Majali, had been injured. Investigators found a bloody sandal at the attack site. With the help of a local citizen, the Yemeni authorities were able to follow his movements to the Saudi-run hospital in Sa'dah and quickly arrested him. Tracking down Fawaz al-Rabi'a and the other conspirators would prove to be more problematic; they were still very much a threat.

When the shooting occurred, I was also heading to Ma'rib but by road.[18] We had made sufficient progress on our projects to justify a return visit to take another look at the regional hospital and explore how we might create a more ambitious development effort there.[19]

While in Ma'rib, I remained in touch with the embassy concerning another dramatic development: the elimination of Abu Ali al-Harithi, al Qaeda's senior leader in Yemen, as a result of cooperation between the Government of Yemen and the United States.[20] The successful operation quickly made the headlines of leading news media. One report stated:

> A missile fired by a U.S. Predator drone over Yemen Sunday [November 3] killed six suspected al Qaeda terrorists in a vehicle about 100 miles east of the nation's capital, the first time the United States has used the unmanned weapon outside Afghanistan. . . .[21]

Subsequent reports provided additional details:

> On November 3, 2002, in Room 3E132, personnel assigned to the [National Security] agency's Special Support Activity, which provides sensitive assistance to military commanders around the world, were in constant touch with a Cryp-

tologic Support Group team in Yemen. The CSG—an NSA in microcosm, designed to be sent to critical areas on short notice—was part of a U.S. National Intelligence Support Team working with Yemeni intelligence officials to try to track down al-Qaeda members. Completing the team were Yemen-based CIA officials and their battery of unmanned Predator drones, each armed with deadly Hellfire missiles, based across the Red Sea in Djibouti. From there, the drones could easily reach anywhere in Yemen.

The CSG team was also patrolling the ether, hunting for any signals linked to its targets. High among those targets was Qaed Salim Sinan al-Harethi [aka Abu Ali al-Harithi], a native Yemeni suspected of belonging to al-Qaeda and planning the attack on the USS *Cole* two years before. But like most of the NSA's new targets, Harethi knew that the United States was searching for him with an electronic dragnet, hoping to snag a brief satellite phone call and determine his location. He carried with him up to five phones—each one, analysts suspect, equipped with multiple cards to change its number. The NSA had a partial list of his numbers and, because Harethi was such a high-priority target, had set up an alarm to go off if any of them was used.[22]

Publicly, the Yemenis put out a cover story. An incident had occurred near Ma'rib. It was thought that the vehicle was transporting a gas canister that had exploded. No link was made to al Qaeda.

Washington could not be discreet. A significant blow had been struck in the war on terror. News of it began to leak, but the articles had vague sourcing that could be absorbed in the static of unending news in the Middle East. However, Deputy Secretary of Defense Paul Wolfowitz was being interviewed by CNN. Much of the interview dealt with the war on terror generally and specifically Indonesia, where he had been ambassador. The incident in Yemen arose. Wolfowitz saw no reason to obfuscate the U.S. role. Acknowledging U.S. involvement, he told the interviewer that "one hopes each time you get a success like that, not only to have gotten rid of somebody dangerous, but to have imposed changes in their tactics and operations and procedures."[23]

A senior American official on CNN directly contradicting the Yemeni cover story produced the predictable effect on the Saleh presidency. I began receiving calls of mounting concern. I quickly communicated that concern to Washington and found sympathy, but little could be done. CNN naturally replayed its Wolfowitz clip again and again, creating an impression, in a country where the government controlled the media, that the U.S. government was insisting on undermining the official Yemeni version. Saleh drew a lesson: while counterterrorism cooperation with the Americans could be effective, it could not be discreet.

The bodies of Abu Ali and his associates were returned to Sanaa for further identification. The interior minister was charged with liaising with the tribes and handing over the remains. The process was particularly sensitive. By Yemeni tribal law and custom, the family of a victim could lodge a blood claim against the party responsible for the death. Abu Ali's clan was large and influential. Such a claim might poison relations between the government and the tribes. I was reliably briefed on the identification and the hand-over. The family representative positively identified Abu Ali and then commented, "He chose his path, and it has led here." His terrorism was a personal affair, not a tribal one.

For Washington, the significance of the operation was underscored by President Bush himself three months later. In his State of the Union address of January 28, 2003, he summed up major counterterrorism accomplishments in the first year following the 9/11 attacks:

> There are days when our fellow citizens do not hear news about the war on terror. There's never a day when I do not learn of another threat, or receive reports of operations in progress or give an order in this global war against a scattered network of killers. The war goes on, and we are winning. To date we have arrested or otherwise dealt with many key commanders of Al Qaida. They include a man who directed logistics and funding for the September the 11th attacks, the chief of Al Qaida operations in the Persian Gulf who planned the bombings of our embassies in East Africa and the USS *Cole*, an Al Qaida operations chief from Southeast Asia, a former director of Al Qaida's training camps in Afghanistan, a key Al Qaida operative in Europe, a major Al Qaida leader in Yemen.[24]

Al Qaeda in Yemen had suffered a staggering blow. Its leader and his key associates had been eliminated. However, Fawaz al-Rabi'a and his associates were still at large and determined to repay—in kind. They would apply the law of the talon, "an eye for an eye," if they could.

CHAPTER SEVEN

THE SEASON OF
ASSASSINATIONS

lthough the Harithi clan reclaimed Abu Ali's body and chose not to exact
a price for his blood, Yemen's political class was much less resigned. The
Yemeni government had put itself in an awkward position. The initial cover
story of an exploding gas canister could not survive CNN's replays of the Wolfowitz
quote. Politicians of the opposition and media seized upon the Yemeni government's
credibility gap and attacked its cooperation with the United States. Eventually, the
government took a new tack: Abu Ali had indeed been a wanted man, and his refusal
to surrender and subject himself to justice had left no alternative. He had met his fate
as a result of a joint Yemeni-U.S. counterterrorism operation. The Americans had
participated at the request of Yemeni authorities who had decided to avail themselves
of American advanced technology in dealing with the wanted man.[1] The rationale had
the merits of truth and logic, but the opposition nevertheless kept up its drumbeat
of criticism. Having gauged the price of its public celebration, Washington belatedly
fell silent.

Unlike the opposition, who focused on the principle of sovereignty, al Qaeda's
remaining operatives decided on a practical response. Fawaz al-Rabi'a was now the
most experienced terrorist in the country. He had organized and executed the bombing campaign against Yemeni security officials the previous spring and the failed attack
on the Hunt helicopter in November. At the prompting of another al Qaeda operative,
Fawzi al-Hababi, he met with a large group, including Fawzi al-Wajeeh, Ibrahim Howaidi, Abdulghani Qifan, Mohamed Saeed, and Qasim al-Raymi. The group "agreed on
assassinating the American Ambassador in Sanaa as a reaction to the assassination of
Abu Ali al-Harithi."[2]

Meanwhile, in December 2002, I was accompanying Foreign Minister al-Qirby on a trip to Washington. It was pleasant duty. The Yemeni-U.S. counterterrorism partnership had finally produced dramatic results. Washington had its scalps. Moreover, Abu Bakr al-Qirby was a consummate diplomat. Fluent in English and politically attuned, he interacted masterfully with members of Washington's interagency process. He also had the advantage of Abdulwahab al-Hajri, Yemen's ambassador to Washington, who was increasingly well connected to a broad range of policymakers. Both proved articulate spokesmen in arguing Yemen's counterterrorism commitment, which had been given credence by Saleh's deeds.

My priorities tended to the mundane: to move resources stuck in the Washington bureaucracy. With excruciating difficulty, the Yemenis were keeping their part of the Oval Office bargain. Now the United States needed to step up and provide assistance. With all my interlocutors, I argued strongly for Yemen to be included in the pending supplemental legislation funding the war on terror. State had proposed the modest sum of $25 million: $20 million in foreign military funds and $5 million in economic support funds. In our Plan Ma'rib, we had requested $200 million in economic funds alone. I made the case at State but also asked NSC officials to weigh in. I knew Afghanistan would get the lion's share, but where in the Middle East, I wondered, could money be better spent in defeating al Qaeda?

I returned again to the Eisenhower Executive Office Building where I found an interested and supportive successor to Clarke in Gen. Wayne Downing. His deputy, Rand Beers, and I had known each other for more than a decade, and he, too, actively supported our counterterrorism efforts.[3]

The fourteen-hour flight back to Sanaa was almost enjoyable. Al-Qirby's meetings had gone exceptionally well. I believed that I had found sympathy for my resource requests. Yemen continued to hold the attention of senior-level officials in Washington if judged by the meetings we had had. Not bad, I reflected, for a country usually on the margins of Washington policymakers' mental maps.

Loyally, Alan Misenheimer, who had replaced Brad Hanson as deputy chief of mission, was at planeside when the Yemenia Airways flight touched down in the very early morning of December 1. He would have been there in any case, but in this instance he had pressing business. During my transit, a Spanish warship, acting on behalf of the U.S.-led coalition, had intercepted a North Korean ship, the *So San*, and found concealed in its cargo Scud missiles apparently bound for Yemen.[4] Our concern with the missile delivery was multifold. First, the shipment was hidden, and therefore it was unclear for whom the missiles were intended. Some thought the ultimate destination might be an enemy such as Iraq or a terrorist group. Second, weapon deals boosted the economy of North Korea, a country President Bush had included in the "Axis of Evil." Third, missile proliferation risked undermining stability in the Middle East. The Yemenis were upset. I had a meeting with the foreign minister to explain the operation early that morning.

Our days in Yemen started seven hours before those in Washington. I had my instructions from Washington to get both the Yemeni side of the story and an early meeting with the foreign minister, so there was little more to do but make the fifteen-minute drive from the airport to the embassy and rest some.

Foreign Minister al-Qirby was as gracious in the crisis as he had been in Washington. I relayed to him the good impression his visit had created, and we then passed to the matter at hand. As noted subsequently by the White House spokesman, the foreign minister confirmed that the shipment in question was a legitimate purchase by Yemen, which did not intend to transfer the missiles to a third party. He was clear that the missiles were Yemeni, and Yemen wanted them delivered.[5]

My cable reporting the meeting had ample time to reach Washington—State and NSC—by opening of business. Rather unusually, Secretary Powell seemed to have had a light morning, so the day's crisis, often delegated to competent assistants, received his personal attention. This was clear in the phone calls I was receiving from NEA. Later I realized that concern extended well beyond State. Friends in NSC related that the president, vice president, and their staffs had engaged as well.

The key questions in Washington's minds were: Does Yemen claim the missiles? Does Yemen really want the missiles? My report made crystal clear the Yemeni claim and desire. As noted in the White House briefing on the incident, Secretary Powell phoned Foreign Minister al-Qirby to test whether the Yemenis might be willing to forgo the missiles in exchange for compensation from the United States. The answer was a firm no. As noted by the White House press spokesman, Vice President Cheney also engaged.[6]

Washington's interest in combating Scud proliferation was large. Its interest in countering terrorism was larger. Moreover, the lawyers could find no legal basis for a seizure.[7] The decision was rightly made to allow the ship to proceed to Aden and to unload the missiles.[8]

No ambassador—at least not I—would seek a crisis such as the So San affair. Had not the secretary, vice president, and president reacted so decisively and wisely, a confrontation over the Scuds might well have poisoned the bilateral relationship and further weakened our newfound partner in Sanaa. In the event, Saleh emerged from the incident with a much-needed political boost.[9] His opponents had portrayed him as an American lackey who had compromised Yemeni sovereignty by allowing the Predator to fly over Yemen and strike terrorists. Saleh had now demonstrated his independence and prevailed over the world's superpower on an issue of disagreement. The crisis provided him breathing room. To retain the initiative, he asked the Ministry of Interior to begin to prepare a white paper on terrorism in Yemen.[10]

It was now Ramadan, the Islamic month of fasting from sunrise to sunset. In most Islamic countries, the religious obligation is taken as an excuse to minimize business and to watch the moon wane slowly until the new crescent is seen and the feast of 'Id al-Fitr begins. In Yemen, town-dwellers also took advantage of the holiday to return to distant villages, which often entailed days of travel by car, by bus, and sometimes on foot.

Al Qaeda's remaining operatives were not slacking off. Rather surprisingly, we found the Yemeni security services also willing to train and conduct operations. When one of the latter resulted in the arrest of Dr. Abu Hurrayah, we exulted. We knew him to be extremely active in plotting what appeared to be a vehicle attack, which we assumed was directed at our embassy. He had procured cars from Oman that appeared to be undergoing "modifications."

Meanwhile, media reports again created turbulence. On December 19, Pat Tyler wrote a story for the *New York Times* in which Yemen was characterized as an unreliable ally. Saleh himself was described as "a volatile army commander."[11] The presidency's reaction was strongly negative. It was true that the Yemeni media regularly pilloried both President Bush and me. On one occasion, those attacks had official sourcing, and the article had clearly been intended to express presidential dissatisfaction with my conduct.[12] Now, Saleh had been made uncomfortable by candid reporting in the American media. As best I could determine, the comment reflected frank talk about the relationship rather than a political message from Washington.

Meanwhile, Secretary Rumsfeld had created a Joint Task Force to deal with terrorism in the Horn of Africa. Yemen was wisely included in the area of operation. In the State Department, the lines that divided the geographic bureaus proved unreasonably hard to cross in doing diplomatic business. The Near East bureau tended to focus on the Arab-Israeli peace process and the Gulf. The Africa bureau rarely looked eastward to the Arabian Peninsula, even though East African countries had significant popula-

The author meets with President Ali Abdullah Saleh in the Presidential Palace. *Courtesy of the Presidency*

The tower houses of a Yemeni village situated for security. *Photo by author*

Bab al-Yemen, the heart of old Sanaa. *Photo by author*

The wisdom of Presidential Adviser Abdulkarim al-Iryani shaped Yemeni-U.S. relations. Note the qamariya window at the top in the background. The qamariya became the emblem of Yemeni-U.S. development efforts. *U.S. Embassy, Sanaa*

Vice President Dick Cheney with President Saleh during Cheney's March 2002 visit. *U.S. Embassy, Sanaa*

American wheat being offloaded by Yemeni stevedores in Al Hudaydah port. *Photo by author*

While the author (white hat) and local officials look on, his wife, Amal, cements the cornerstone of the museum in Ma'rib. Note the qamariya emblem that identifies Yemeni-U.S. development projects. *U.S. Embassy, Sanaa*

The Ministry of Health could find few health professionals willing to serve in Ma'rib, so local youths were recruited, educated in Sanaa, and returned home. *U.S. Embassy, Sanaa*

The young shepherdesses who controlled most of Ma'rib's livestock wealth were the focus of an agricultural extension project. The author talks with two graduates. Embassy development expert Gareth Harries is to the right of the author. *U.S. Embassy, Sanaa*

Travels in Ma'rib, Al Jawf, and Shabwah were often off-road but always safeguarded by Ministry of Interior's dishkas. With such protection and prudence, embassy personnel traveled throughout Yemen. *Photo by author*

tions of Muslims oriented toward Saudi Arabia. Al Qaeda valued the connections and had used them effectively to attack our embassies in Nairobi and Dar es Salaam. I therefore welcomed the U.S. military's effort to cover this political seam.

Maj. Gen. John Sattler was designated to stand up the task force. An associate from Clarke's Counterterrorism Security Group, he was an outstanding choice. Shortly before Christmas, he visited Yemen on the initial tour of his area of responsibility. Saleh was in Al Hudaydah following a trip to frigid Moscow. We found his staff suffering from colds, and Saleh was initially not pleased to see us. The taste of the Tyler story was still in his mouth. However, when General Sattler began to talk about an international effort to monitor and, to some extent, control illegal traffic between the Arabian Peninsula and the Horn of Africa, Saleh perked up. Yemen, as impoverished as it was, still attracted large numbers of illegal immigrants wishing to settle there or move north to Saudi Arabia. As matters stood, the Yemenis usually discovered these refugees when they were already ashore or perhaps very near its coast. If the traffic could be interdicted near Africa, then the process would become much more manageable for the Yemenis. Saleh called for maps, and all parties were soon kneeling on the floor as Saleh detailed the troubling immigration routes.

Our attention was soon riveted back to terrorism. On December 30, gunmen attacked the American Baptist hospital in Jiblah, south of Sanaa and midway to Aden. They killed three American staff members: Bill Koehn, Dr. Martha Myers, and Kathy Gariety. A fourth employee, Donald Caswell, was shot and seriously injured, but survived.[13] We and the Yemenis were shocked. The hospital had been an institution in the region for decades. Koehn, the hospital administrator, had worked in Yemen for twenty-seven years, Dr. Myers for twenty-four, and Gariety for almost a decade. I had visited the hospital early in my tenure and found a modest facility staffed by extraordinarily dedicated individuals. Ironically, the Baptist Missions headquarters back in the United States had already decided it could no longer support the undertaking, and the facility's transfer to the Ministry of Health was scheduled within the year.

The assailant, Abdel Razzak Kamal, was a young man who had been treated at the hospital on several occasions. Familiar with procedures there, which included virtually no security, he easily brought a gun into the main building and waited until his primary target, Dr. Myers, joined several other colleagues in a meeting. He then forced his entry into the administrative office, shot Dr. Myers, and then the others. Having exhausted his ammunition, the assailant surrendered. The embassy rushed a team to Jiblah to assist the victims and bring remaining Americans to Sanaa for safekeeping.[14]

Again, NCIS and FBI investigators went in with the first wave.[15] The FBI scrupulously followed the case and helped ensure successful prosecution and punishment.

Nearly simultaneously, Kamal's mentor, Ali Jarallah, undertook a separate attack in Sanaa. His target was Jarallah Omar, secretary-general of the Yemeni Socialist Party, one of Yemen's three major political parties. Omar was shot to death while a guest at the annual conference of Islah, Yemen's second largest party, headed by Sheikh Abdullah al-Ahmar.

The two plots had no connection with al Qaeda. Homegrown extremists had concocted a long list of enemies who included socialists, missionaries, and so-called heretics.[16] As a result, public opinion dominated by the Predator controversy swung sharply in a new direction. There was an outpouring of sympathy for the American victims, the more so as they were known to be unselfishly serving the needs of poor Yemenis. And the opposition Socialist Party suddenly found itself a victim of terrorism. The opposition Islamic party, Islah, was embarrassed by a terrorist act at a venue under its control. The harm to the victims, who were in some way guests in both cases, violated tribal norms.

Within days, Interior Minister al-Alimi presented to the Parliament the government's white paper—a ninety-five-page document titled *Terror in Yemen*, which had been under preparation to explain the Predator operation. For the first time, the Yemeni government took the initiative in detailing past terrorist attacks, their negative impact, and its policy of cooperation on counterterrorism. The document was both factual and amply illustrated with crime-scene photos. It successfully redefined the Predator incident as reasonable counterterrorism cooperation between partners. In the wave of public revulsion caused by the attacks in Jiblah and Sanaa, the Yemeni parliament and public overwhelmingly embraced the government's position. Criticism waned.

The U.S.-Yemeni counterterrorism relationship ended 2002 in better shape than any of us could have expected a year previously: al Qaeda's leader in Yemen had been removed, counterterrorism cooperation and training was progressing, and the government's public diplomacy campaign with the Yemeni people had regained the high moral ground. In the Middle East, such progress is rarely sustained. When matters go well, it is well to expect problems. And so it was.

The FBI had long been tracking the relationship between American Muslims and Yemeni sheikh Mohammed Ali Hassan al-Moayad. We soon learned that he might be arrested for material support to a terrorist organization with the cooperation of the Germans following a meeting arranged by an informant in Frankfurt. We scurried to locate the sheikh on our political radar. It turned out that while he had no government status, he was an influential Islah member and extremely popular in Sanaa as a result of good works performed at his mosque complex, which included a bakery that produced bread for the poor.

The sheikh was well known for his support for Hamas, the Palestinian group whose members were seen as resistance fighters by the vast majority of Yemenis and as terrorists by the U.S. and European governments. He was also, we had discovered, possibly implicated with al Qaeda. In private conversations, he boasted of his relationship with Osama bin Laden and of providing funding to al Qaeda. His name had appeared "in pocket litter" in Afghanistan, which lent credence to these claims.

Al-Moayad's arrest by German authorities and subsequent extradition to the United States were met with a firestorm of criticism in Yemen. Both popular and official opinion swung firmly behind him owing to his philanthropy. Because his primary association was with Hamas, not al Qaeda, the American case had little credibility.[17]

Even though the disagreement on al-Moayad soured the mood, it did not destroy cooperation. In March, after long urging, the Yemenis detained al Qaeda associate Hedi Dulkim in Sa'dah, not far from the Saudi border. Initially, we had identified Dulkim as a minor player in the al Qaeda organization. However, interrogation of Abd al-Rahim al-Nashiri, now in U.S. custody, revealed that he played a key role in facilitating the smuggling of operatives and weapons between Yemen and Saudi Arabia. The Yemenis cited Dulkim's arrest as evidence that the government was serious in pursuing al Qaeda operatives. At the same time, they acknowledged that Fawaz al-Rabi'a, al Qaeda's most dangerous operative in Yemen, remained at large.

On March 18, Hunt Oil also lost three employees, including Ronald Horsch of Texas, in a shooting at a production site near Ma'rib. Again, the Yemenis welcomed U.S. assistance in the investigation, which revealed the incident not to be a terrorist act, but that of a deranged employee on medication who was convinced that he was being persecuted as a homosexual.

Operation Iraqi Freedom, launched on March 20, 2003, then impacted on Yemen and throughout the Middle East. Saleh had consistently counseled us against a military invasion of Iraq. Even as we discussed continuing progress in counterterrorism, notably Dulkim's arrest, Saleh repeated his counsel. Yemen, he quipped, remained focused on counterterrorism while the United States was becoming preoccupied with Iraq. I noted the recent arrest of 9/11 mastermind Khalid Sheikh Mohammed as evidence that we continue our counterterrorism efforts even as we prepared to confront

Saddam. Saleh made a long, impassioned plea against the invasion. I countered that he should look ahead to Iraq five years after Saddam had been removed and also noted that the Gulf States, particularly Kuwait, were extremely supportive. Saleh remained unconvinced, consistently opposed the invasion, and predicted great problems as a result of the coming war. At the same time, he provided assurances that Yemen would continue to cooperate in counterterrorism and protect all Americans in Yemen. As a safety valve to vent popular frustration, antiwar demonstrations would be allowed, but they would be kept peaceful.

To me, Saleh's position was reasonable. It reflected genuine personal misgivings about our course of action in Iraq and also a political imperative: in the midst of the electoral campaign for the Yemeni parliament, the ruling party could not hand Iraq to the opposition as an issue. Saleh's position also demonstrated that he had learned a powerful lesson from the first Gulf War when Yemen had voted against Operation Desert Storm. That vote had cost the Yemenis dearly in economic and security assistance from the United States and Arab Gulf states. Saleh was now moving Yemen to the sidelines in order to safeguard its interests.

Operation Iraqi Freedom released the genie from the lamp. In Yemen demonstrators took to the streets, intensifying protests that had been going on in the lead-up to the military action. While the embassy remained on high alert, we were reassured by Saleh's commitment, the peaceful nature of previous protests, and the reinforced security measures around the embassy, which I personally reviewed as tensions mounted.

On March 21, demonstrators gathered in Tahrir Square in central Sanaa, several miles from the American embassy. Unlike previous marches, however, this one headed toward the embassy. Leading members of the Yemeni Ba'ath Party, loyal to Saddam, had decided to seize control of this march and use it to confront the embassy. As in the past, the Yemeni security forces allowed the march to proceed since it appeared peaceful. However, when the march reached the Sheraton traffic circle, a block from the embassy, the security services drew a line. We monitored events from the embassy. Our own security personnel on the roofs could see the demonstrators, and we received regular reports from our surveillance detection team circulating outside.

We could not know whether the Yemeni security services would hold the line. We were also concerned about small groups that broke off from the main demonstration and attempted to circumvent the security forces and reach our perimeter. In the embassy, only essential personnel were on duty, and they had been centralized in the main chancery building. I walked around quickly to survey preparations. Our Marines were in full battle gear. Col. Scott Duke, head of our temporary-duty training detachment, was calmly slipping bullets into the magazine of his assault rifle. A great deal, I thought, is riding on Col. Yahya Saleh's security forces. We were balanced on the knife's edge.

The demonstrators confronted the Yemeni security force, which held its ground. Unfortunately, they were ill equipped and ill trained for crowd control. Their water cannon had limited effect. Then a shot was fired from among the demonstrators. There were also reports of demonstrators launching grenades. The Yemeni forces returned fire in a deliberate manner. Two demonstrators were killed, including a young boy.[18] The security forces remained disciplined. Confronted by their firmness, the demonstrators began to disperse. We could see the demonstration breaking up from our rooftop vantage points. Our teams outside confirmed that impression, and the embassy internal defense team stood down. President Saleh had kept his promise.

In the wake of the violent demonstration of March 21, he called together his security team. The organizers of the violence were arrested, and demonstrations were banned. Through Mohamed Suddam, the president passed renewed assurances of embassy protection. The security forces performance lent them credibility.

Although the embassy had been the target of the demonstration, we knew all Americans were vulnerable. We advised them of the incident and recommended they avoid crowds and move about as little as possible. Within a week, the situation had stabilized sufficiently enough that I gathered our wardens in the embassy for an update.[19] We were also comparing notes with our diplomatic colleagues. A European ambassador who was a close friend asked to see me that afternoon.

As usual, I found our wardens well connected through their own networks and remarkably calm. I valued their perspective and was prepared to spend as long with them as useful. Hence, I received, but did not respond to, a note announcing my diplomatic colleague's arrival in my office. After perhaps a quarter of an hour, Sandy, my secretary, marched into view in back of the audience. Pointing to her watch, she made clear that I was in serious breach of protocol in keeping my counterpart waiting. She was determined that such behavior—even by the ambassador—would not happen on her watch.

I excused myself and proceeded to my office where he was waiting patiently. Without the slightest hint of annoyance, he proceeded to relate a strange and troubling story. A "friend" of his embassy had approached its security personnel on behalf of an Iraqi who claimed to be a member of a cell run by the Iraqi Intelligence Service. That cell was targeting American diplomats in response to the invasion.

I asked for my security staff to join us, and my colleague repeated his information. We decided it best if we could convince his contact to come to the embassy for debriefing. We asked an NCIS officer, a native Arabic speaker, to make the invitation in a telephone call. He proved convincing, and the source was soon being professionally debriefed. His information was alarming but precise and credible. He also had sketchy information about plots elsewhere in the Middle East.

We immediately brought our targeted personnel into the embassy for safekeeping,[20] and notified Washington and Yemeni authorities. Based on the information, the Yemeni authorities acted in the early hours of the morning, arrested the cell members, and found sophisticated bombs.

Deputy Assistant Secretary Ryan Crocker was soon in touch, reporting that the informant's information had also led to the arrest of cells in two other Middle East countries. Washington had expected Iraq to respond to the invasion with their terrorist assets. That response had now been detected and countered, and the embassy in Yemen got credit. I asked that Secretary Powell send a message to thank the government of my diplomatic colleague for his cooperation. My colleague and I also decided to partner in the Sanaa duplicate bridge club where we continued a most productive relationship. However, no one was more gratified than Sandy. Never again did she have to worry about me keeping a diplomatic colleague cooling his heels.

Still, al Qaeda operatives remained at large, and I was their target. At the time, we had no specific threat information. Nevertheless, Regional Security Officer Tim Laas was continually enhancing the embassy's security and mine. In the wake of the Predator attack, we decided to augment my personal security. The Diplomatic Security bureau in the State Department deployed trainers, and Laas picked some of the best and brightest from among the local guard force employed by the embassy. My personal bodyguard was chosen to coordinate the force.

Not surprisingly, their mission put them squarely in harm's way. The al Qaeda assassination group had done its homework. Ibrahim Howaidi, Abdulghani Qifan, and Qasim al-Raymi had monitored my movements. On leaving the embassy, my motorcade either turned right toward the Sheraton traffic circle or left to a similar intersection. At these choke points, the group determined to strike. Their plans called for a bomb, a small-arms ambush, or a rocket attack. They were prepared for a hard, armored target. Fawzi al-Hababi undertook to procure the weapons.

Before the attack could be launched, however, the Yemeni security services located Fawaz al-Rabi'a and his brother, Abu Bakr, long sought for their roles in the bombings at PSO locations the previous spring. The two brothers were confronted at a location in the Mathbah district of Sanaa.[21] They resisted with submachine guns and grenades, and escaped. With Hizam al-Majali, they fled in a rented vehicle south. At the security checkpoint at Al Arqub, a PSO officer asked for identification, which Fawaz al-Rabi'a did not have. The officer climbed aboard the vehicle and instructed the driver to proceed to Aden to confirm Fawaz al-Rabi'a's identity. On the way, Fawaz al-Rabi'a wrested the officer's gun from him, and al-Majali shot and killed him. Again, they escaped.

Eventually, however, an alert citizen informed the security services of al-Rabi'a's location. He and the other plotters were captured. The enhanced security measures continued, but none of my guards had to take a bullet, bomb, or rocket on my behalf.

CHAPTER EIGHT

AN EMBASSY,
NOT A BUNKER

In Yemen, counterterrorism began with securing our own base of operations and our people. We hardened our embassy and trained our personnel to make them difficult targets. Al Qaeda's operations against us, although never precluded, were made problematic. In the end, their choice to attack the embassy by a rocket instead of a vehicle bomb meant they probably would not have caused mass casualties even had they succeeded in launching their operation. We could have adopted even greater security measures by reducing staff and our activity.

The State Department's Bureau of Diplomatic Security tended to favor this approach and fought hard to keep the embassy staff limited in number. Authorized departure became the symbol of this approach. By strictly limiting the embassy staffing to "essential" personnel, the security experts understandably sought to avoid the kind of casualties to embassy dependents we had suffered in Islamabad in 2002.[1] As ambassador, I saw significant costs to this narrow approach and the real possibility that it would cripple our counterterrorism effort. We needed to engage the Yemenis on many fronts, including economic development. I needed staff to do so. Yet, because of authorized departure and years of attrition in State Department staffing, Embassy Sanaa during the first critical year had no USAID representation, no economic section, and no public diplomacy section.

Secretary of State Powell, I felt, had expressed a much healthier attitude in our initial briefing on the al Qaeda threat in December 2000. He had concluded the session by noting that terrorism was to be taken very seriously but that the United States would not "hunker down." Rather, we would deal with terrorism and also conduct our diplomacy. Unfortunately, the decision-making process in State did not reflect this attitude, but rather put risk-averse officials in the Office of Management largely in charge. Overcoming their aversion to risk and recruiting necessary staff was a major challenge.[2]

Diplomacy formed the basis for counterterrorism cooperation in Yemen, and the embassy's political agenda did receive significant help from visitors. We took our guidance on visitors from Will Rogers: we never met one we didn't like. Some came with unfocused agendas, which allowed us to propose our own lens with which to view the al Qaeda threat and U.S. interests. A few nodded sympathetically in response to Yemeni requests—outrageous and otherwise—which left us to correct Yemeni expectations. But, on the whole, the embassy benefited enormously from those American officials who took the time and ran the security gauntlet that led to Sanaa.

One such visitor, Wendy Chamberlin, helped us to address the embassy's critical deficit in development talent. A former ambassador to Pakistan, Wendy visited in her new capacity as assistant administrator for USAID. She immediately seized the connection we proposed between security and development, and returned to Washington to fight our bureaucratic battle. In 2002 the U.S. embassy in Sanaa had improvised its development program, including the initiative to focus our efforts on the tribal areas. We had relied on the embassy's Yemeni staff, particularly Ahmed Attieg, Shaif al-Hamdany, and Fawzia Yousef, as well as the highly professional staff of the Social Fund and the Public Works Project. Our appetite for development work, however, far exceeded our resources.

Wendy's efforts culminated in 2003 in the reestablishment of USAID in Yemen after a seven-year hiatus. Doug Heisler, a development professional, took charge of the embassy program and provided remarkable leadership. Uncharacteristically, Doug did not limit his vision to sustainable development, which has been USAID's traditional mission. Rather, he embraced the concept of development as linked to security.[3] Doug also deftly managed a "friendly acquisition" of existing programs and staff, including the 416b projects funded by U.S. agricultural surpluses, which normally fell outside of USAID's purview. To professionalize our operation, he drew up a set of "development assistance programming principles," which guided all our activities. As deputy chief of mission in Cairo in the 1990s, then the largest USAID operation in the world, I knew that Congress imposed extremely tight controls over taxpayers' money used for development. With Doug in Sanaa, I was confident for the first time that our programs could survive such scrutiny.

Upon my arrival in September 2001, the embassy's public diplomacy section was a ghost town. Its work had been deemed "nonessential," and its American employees had departed. The Yemeni staff was willing but not able to undertake the culturally taxing mission of explaining U.S. foreign policy on the Middle East or counterterrorism. Embassy Sanaa represented an extreme case of a larger problem. At Senator Jesse Helms's insistence, the U.S. Information Agency (USIA) had been incorporated into the State Department during the '90s. While the move made perfect management sense, it submerged USIA's distinctive culture, which valued highly public diplomacy and cultural exchange, into State's culture, which prized policymaking and official diplomacy. Their mission neglected, USIA's ranks had been demoralized in the process.

To get Sanaa's program back on track, we reached back into the golden age of USIA and recruited Boulos Malik, a legendary figure and still active in his retirement. State had usefully adopted a practice of creating a reserve corps of Foreign Service officers who could be paid "when actually employed." Called WAEs, they were our salvation during the critical year 2001–2 and none more so than Boulos in reviving our public diplomacy. Boulos's native Arabic skills and long experience gave the embassy an effective voice in dealing with Yemen's contentious media

After his departure, another Arabic speaker, John Balian, came aboard and significantly broadened and deepened our relations with Yemeni media, academics, and officials. John set up a workshop on photojournalism, for example. On its initial day, some forty young Yemeni journalists showed up, but then a negative development in the Middle East prompted the journalist syndicate to announce a boycott. I asked John whether we should cancel the program, and he said no. As previously scheduled, I met with the group the following day for a dialogue on U.S. policy. As John had expected, almost all of the participating Yemenis returned in defiance of the boycott and prepared for a spirited debate.

For our purposes, we had to convince the Yemeni government and eventually the public that cooperation with the United States on counterterrorism was in Yemen's interest as well as ours. Saleh and his public diplomacy team were the most important actors in this regard. In the wake of his travels to Washington, Saleh adopted the theme that terrorism was a threat to Yemen and that cooperation with international partners, including the United States, served its interests.

For our part, we were well served with the messages that I had proposed in my initial public remarks. First, I insisted that Yemen was a partner, not a target, in the war on terror. Second, I insisted on the link between the Yemenis' economic ambition and cooperation on counterterrorism: "No development without security; no security without development." The embassy's public diplomacy efforts were instrumental in creating an atmosphere in which Yemeni officials, citizens, and nongovernmental organizations could work with Americans toward common goals. However, our public diplomacy could not win the battle for the Yemeni "heart and mind." That task fell to the Yemeni government.

In Egypt in the mid-1990s, the Egyptians confronted a similar challenge during the fierce terrorism campaign of the Egyptian Islamic Jihad and al Gama'at al Islamiyya.[4] Then, the tipping point occurred when the terrorists inadvertently killed a twelve-year-old Egyptian girl, who came to symbolize the innocent victims of terrorism. Similarly, in Yemen I believe the public sentiment tipped against al Qaeda when it attacked the M/V *Limburg* off Al Mukalla. The French tanker had no military or security significance. The victims in its attack were Yemeni fishermen whose fishing beds were polluted and Yemeni workers whose livelihoods were connected with the port and oil. The Saleh government did an extraordinarily good job in bringing home this message. Al Qaeda never recovered the moral high ground.

Arabic was an essential skill across the board. Although mine was far from eloquent, it served well for dialogue with the Yemenis and in periodic encounters with the Yemeni media, which were almost always in Arabic. My first deputy, Brad Hanson, spoke good Arabic as well, whereas his successor Alan Misenheimer's Arabic was more than adequate, and he used it with relish. The embassy's best Arabic came from Boulos Malik and later Nabil Khoury when he succeeded Alan as deputy chief of mission in 2004. Arabic became a hallmark of the embassy, from the ambassador down to our many entry-level Foreign Service officers, who rightly identified Sanaa as an ideal environment in which to learn and use the language.

American law enforcement personnel—the FBI and NCIS—provided critical assistance in the embassy's counterterrorism operations. Because of the USS *Cole*, both institutions had dedicated significant resources to Yemen. As noted above, their most effective agents were Arab Americans who brought fluent Arabic and cultural sensitivity to their collaboration with the Yemenis.

From my experiences in Egypt in the mid-1990s, I was familiar with the rivalry between the CIA and FBI on matters related to counterterrorism. At that time, the FBI had begun to establish legal attachés at selected U.S. missions to promote international cooperation on law enforcement. The embassy's intelligence representatives opposed the proposal vigorously, and progress was painful until a senior U.S. official paid a visit. In a meeting that included all parties, he decreed that "spies make bad cops, and cops make bad spies," so we needed both.

I agreed wholeheartedly. American law enforcement personnel in Yemen had done a spectacular job in investigating the attack on the *Cole*. Taken together with their findings in the East Africa embassy bombings, they were able to evolve a sophisticated picture of al Qaeda and its operations. This familiarity with its operators also allowed them to establish the first solid link between the perpetrators of the 9/11 attacks and the terrorist organization.

The *Cole* sites in Aden, the Al Qadissiyya site of the August 2002 missile misfire, and the Al Mukalla sites associated with the M/V *Limburg* attack all provided valuable insights into al Qaeda's links and operations. The two agencies operated seamlessly, and I was particularly impressed by NCIS's professionalism and deference to the FBI, which acted as the lead investigator.

I also needed the FBI to build relations with Interior Minister al-Alimi and his ministry. The intelligence liaison naturally connected our intelligence services, but we had no natural counterpart for the Ministry of Interior. And yet, al-Alimi largely controlled investigations of terrorist acts and commanded the CSF, which had a significant counterterrorist mission. FBI agents in Sanaa on temporary duty had succeeded in establishing some rapport, but I continued to push for a legal attaché. Since few individuals in the Ministry of Interior spoke English, I strongly preferred an Arabic speaker. Unfortunately, the FBI had only a handful of Arabic-speaking agents, and they were in demand from New York to Islamabad. I harassed Washington and thus added to the overwhelming burden already being carried by Director Mueller.[5]

The U.S. military had a robust presence in Embassy Sanaa. They provided analysts, planners, operators, civil affairs specialists, and trainers. From Washington, there was a great deal of pressure to move to combat operations in Yemen, particularly in 2002. Following our success in Afghanistan and prior to the draining commitment of Iraq, some favored using "kinetic" approaches more generally, and Yemen appeared a likely theater.

CENTCOM planners preferred massive firepower. The weapon of choice might be cruise missiles, aerial bombs, or an AC-130 gunship. Inevitably, there would have been heavy collateral casualties. U.S. special operations forces were theoretically a more surgical option, but planning always entailed options for massive support for the special forces should they become trapped. U.S. military requirements of the Yemeni side in a collaborative arrangement were far-reaching indeed. Unilateral U.S. action was fraught with difficulties: unfamiliar terrain, difficulty in identifying targets, and remote locations that were not accessible discreetly. Direct U.S. military involvement was fraught with risks.

As a consequence, the U.S. military's more significant contribution to counterterrorism in Yemen was training the CSF, which was willing and, with training, able to engage al Qaeda. One key to success of counterterrorism in Yemen was the training and successful deployments of these forces, especially in 2003–4.

The U.S. Coast Guard also played a notable and successful role, resulting in the Yemeni Coast Guard Plan delivered in April 2002. Capt. Jim Willis then unfortunately was tapped to organize training for the Transportation Security Administration, which was taking over responsibilities at American airports. I despaired at finding a comparable replacement but was surprised to find in Capt. Bob Innis a rare talent. Bob undertook the even more difficult task of implementing the coast guard plan and masterfully maneuvered in both Sanaa and Washington to realize our vision. When other aspects of counterterrorism were not moving or, worse, moving in the wrong direction, I could always schedule a briefing on the project by Bob to renew my faith that progress was possible. His work came to fruition with the commissioning of the Yemeni Coast Guard squadron in Aden on April 7, 2004.

In his second inaugural address, President Bush solemnly announced that "it is the policy of the United States to seek and support the growth of democratic movements and institutions in every nation and culture, with the ultimate goal of ending tyranny in our world." While it became a doctrine in the second term, promoting reform and democracy was, in fact, actively pursued in the first term as well. Assistant Secretary of State Bill Burns promoted a "positive agenda" in the Middle East, which was made tangible through MEPI. As noted above, we in Sanaa embraced this initiative wholeheartedly and led the region in grants in its first year. Happily, MEPI coincided with Secretary Powell's Diplomatic Readiness Initiative, which brought a wave of talented young officers into the Foreign Service.[6] In Sanaa, they came to work on public diplomacy, development, and promoting democracy and human rights, as well as consular duties. Many, like Cathy Westley, were veterans of nongovernmental organizations. Cathy had worked previously for the National Democratic Institute (NDI), which was also working in Yemen under the leadership of Dr. Robin Madrid. Robin's most important work focused on reform of the Yemeni electoral system and development of Yemen's political parties.

Finally, with modification in the embassy's authorized departure status, my wife, Amal, was able to join me in March 2003. A Palestinian from Jerusalem, she felt equally at home in the capital of Sanaa or a remote area of Al Jawf. She was both an Islamic art historian and a former curator of the museum of one of Islam's most sacred shrines, the Haram al-Sharif in Jerusalem. She brought to her activities in Yemen deep appreciation for its culture. To her goes much of the credit for conceiving the archaeological museum project in Ma'rib and in realizing Yemen's extremely successful exhibit—"Windows on Yemen"—which attracted standing-room-only crowds to the Smithsonian Institution's Freer Gallery of Art in Washington in early September 2003. Not the least of her accomplishments was convincing both the Yemeni government and business community to make modest investments to bring Yemen's rich cultural heritage to the world's attention.

The defining characteristic, then, across the spectrum of our activity was engagement. Embassy officers seized initiatives and used a secure embassy as a platform for engaging with Yemenis not only in the capital, but throughout the country. We rejected both the embassy as bunker and the proposition that any part of Yemen was a "no-go" zone. To do otherwise would have conceded to al Qaeda the initiative and safe haven.

CHAPTER NINE

NOTHING IS AS GOOD
AS IT SEEMS

I n the Middle East, progress is never linear. There is always a dip, often a reversal. And so it was in Yemen as we entered 2003 with the counterterrorism relationship productive and al Qaeda on the run.

My friends in Washington always saw the backsliding as a Yemeni phenomenon. I personally felt the Yemenis could have accused us of inconstancy as well. As Yemeni security forces, aided by their citizens, were closing in on Fawaz al-Rabi'a, the Washington decision makers were finalizing the president's 2003 supplemental. This was the appropriation to fund the war on terror. The president had repeatedly recognized Yemen as a significant front in that war. His six-month progress report to Congress in March 2002 had cited Yemen by name as one of three specific fronts on which we were engaged following 9/11. In his 2003 State of the Union address, the president had similarly cited the elimination of Abu Ali as one of the campaign's most significant accomplishments.

The administration had originally requested $25 million in military and economic funding for Yemen in the emergency supplemental—a modest sum compared to the billions our military was spending. But in late March, the Near East bureau informed us the funds had been deleted. Overwhelmingly, the money had gone to Jordan: $406 million out of $907.5 million.[1] The allocations were consistent with a larger pattern. In the regular appropriations, resources overwhelmingly would continue to be channeled to Israel, Egypt, and Jordan. In the words of an Office of Management and Budget explanation, "in order to provide required levels for Israel and Egypt, as well as sufficient resources for Jordan, State and USAID will have to constrain assistance funding for other countries in the region that are lower priorities in the war on terrorism."[2]

In my admittedly parochial view, 9/11 should have changed our priorities, and those new priorities should have dictated allocation of resources. In fact, little had changed. The old priorities stemming from our long-standing and admirable commitment to building peace between Israel and the Arabs prevailed in the Near East Bureau. We talked about bringing all instruments of national power into the struggle against terrorism, but we did not walk that talk.[3] For our initial effort in Yemen, the normal channels of funding would be largely denied us. We would have to fashion our tool kit from wherever possible: food assistance, MEPI, and other agencies' funding. Necessity demanded that we be inventive.

Our case for the U.S.-Yemeni partnership then received a jolt in Yemen. In April there was a disturbing rumor from Aden, where Public Affairs Officer John Balian had excellent relations with journalists. He brought me a report that on April 11, ten suspects in the USS *Cole* attack had broken out of an Aden jail. We had not even been told of their transfer to Aden. True, as a result of Saleh's appeal to FBI director Mueller, we had finally given a green light to prosecuting the small fry, so a move of these defendants to a trial venue had some logic. However, transferring the ringleader, Jamal al-Badawi, or his associate Fahd al-Quso, was problematic on many levels. Nevertheless, they too were among the transfers and now escapees.

Persistent phone calls finally elicited a sheepish acknowledgement from the Ministry of Interior. The accused had indeed been moved in anticipation of a trial in Aden. Detained in the PSO's facility there, they had managed to dig through a wall and to escape into the night. An investigation was under way. They would be recaptured. The United States shared responsibility for having long delayed their trial, ministry officials argued.

I was less interested in debating the wisdom of trial timing than doing everything possible to recapture individuals with American blood on their hands. I laid down a clear marker that the subject would not go away. It would cast a shadow over our cooperation until they were finally brought to justice. Not a threat—simply a fact.

The following day, the leading Yemeni newspaper, *Al Thawra*, carried a front-page article that included pictures of the ten escapees and the offer of a reward for information leading to their rearrest. Saleh also took a step that indicated something unusual in the Yemeni governmental experience: accountability. Hussein al-Ansi, the PSO's powerful chief in Aden, was detained for questioning and eventually sacked.

To our knowledge, there was no proof of complicity, but at a minimum he had been guilty of gross neglect.

Although buffeted by setbacks in Washington and now in Aden, the embassy team was determined to maintain its bearing. Our pursuit of counterterrorism across a broad spectrum continued. We particularly needed to demonstrate progress in development to complement the clear progress we had made on the security side. Ma'rib was the test case, so I traveled there for the third time on April 20–21. On the health front, we were making substantial progress. The Social Fund had begun construction of the new health center in Madghil, and we had reached agreement with the minister of health to invest $7 million in equipping the large regional hospital in Ma'rib and training its staff. We now looked to expand our development effort in two directions: agriculture and archaeology. The former was evident. Ma'rib had been an agricultural center in antiquity, thanks to the waters stored behind its ancient dam. Currently, its agriculture was suffering from overuse of ground water with increasing salinity. Such water was distributed in open, earthen irrigation channels. Simply replacing those with Yemen-made plastic pipes would decrease wastage by half. We also found the agricultural extension office nonfunctional. Expensive equipment supplied by other donors stood unused because the facility had never been connected to the electrical grid. We determined to finance that connection. We also determined that much of Ma'rib's wealth lay in its herds of sheep and goats, which were generally in the charge of the young women. There was a significant market for Yemen's livestock just across the border in Saudi Arabia. We undertook to fund training courses for ten Yemeni female extension agents.

Ma'rib was also undoubtedly rich in history and archaeology. The Germans had done a thoroughly professional job in excavating and restoring the Bar'an Temple in Ma'rib. The American Foundation for the Study of Man was running a dig at the even larger Mahram Bilqis. All excavations were controversial, however. Many in Ma'rib believed the artifacts found would be taken by foreigners or by the government and removed to Sanaa.[4] We had one credible report that resentment among the young men in a local tribe might lead to kidnapping of archaeologists. A good way to head off a resurgence of kidnapping and boost Ma'rib's long-term economic prospects was to fund a small local museum that would include facilities for treating and preserving artifacts, a capability that American excavators lacked. This kind of tourism development required faith and vision. Amal undertook the project as a labor of love. In the Social Fund, she found a most competent and willing partner.

Even as counterterrorism cooperation suffered its setbacks, the Yemenis did advance on another important front. Saleh had debated postponing the parliamentary elections scheduled for April 27 in light of the turmoil created by the American invasion of Iraq. He wisely allowed them to proceed.

In Yemen the conduct of the elections was in the hands of the Supreme Commission for Elections and Referenda (SCER). Unusually in an Arab country, this body had significant autonomy. Both the ruling party and opposition parties were active in its management. Moreover, SCER effectively tapped international expertise provided by the UN Development Fund, the International Foundation for Election Systems, and, most significantly, the NDI. As NDI's director in Yemen, Dr. Robin Madrid brought both expertise and acute cross-cultural sensitivity to her mission. SCER would hold meetings including international representatives and diplomats to review planning for the elections. Serious issues would be brought up, including voting lists, counting procedures, and code of conduct. Often the chairman would turn to Robin for her views and for a recommended course of action.

NDI was also active with the political parties and ran campaign workshops in Sanaa, Aden, and Al Mukalla. Often it was the opposition parties that took the most advantage of this training. Ironically, the Yemeni women were the most open to modern campaign methods and proved to be effective canvassers. NDI's impartial approach won the respect of all parties, most notably Islah. Washington or the embassy's pronouncements on democracy carried little weight. NDI's activities in promoting democracy, however, carried a great deal.

Violence during the campaign was the major concern, and corruption the major campaign issue. Contrary to expectations, the opposition parties did not attack Saleh's government for its counterterrorism campaign or for its cooperation with the United States. Yemeni government public diplomacy efforts and political missteps by the terrorists had successfully removed counterterrorism activity from the political debate. This was remarkable in itself.

But violence during the registration process and campaigning, and at the polling stations, remained a real and present risk. NDI and the other international advisory groups proposed that all parties subscribe to a code of conduct in order to outlaw violence from the election process. This was agreed. Election day dawned on April 27, and the government and opposition parties decreed a "weapons-free" day. In Yemen, where a Kalashnikov is as ubiquitous as a cell phone in the United States, the proposition of leaving your weapon at home while you went to vote was a stunningly novel idea. Yet, the time had come. Voting took place throughout Yemen with little violence and few casualties.[5]

As voting day had approached, however, the Europeans got cold feet and cancelled their observer delegations.[6] NDI proceeded with its delegation, totaling about thirty observers from eleven nations in North America, Europe, South America, the Middle East, and North Africa. They were an impressive group of political leaders, including present and former elected officials, as well as experts on human rights, election processes, and Yemeni history and politics. They came early (April 22) and stayed late (April 29). To their ranks, the American embassy added a like number of observers, organized and trained by Cathy Westley, an NDI veteran whose first tour as a Foreign Service officer had been to Sanaa. She engendered enthusiasm, and volunteers came from across embassy ranks—consular, administrative, military, public diplomacy, and economic. Minister al-Alimi and his security forces again provided robust protection when called on but generally without intimidation of voters or voting officials.

I visited several polling stations in Sanaa where the opposition was to mount its most successful challenge to the ruling party. I found the voting process unusually well organized. Both opposition and ruling parties were represented on the committees conducting the vote. The registration lists were elaborate, including photos of the voter. Voters presented themselves, identified themselves, voted secretly, and dipped their thumbs in indelible ink. The women's polling was particularly impressive, as efficient as the voting I had done in my precinct in Falls Church, Virginia.

Irregularities occurred to be sure. NDI's report on the election did not mince words. There was evidence in numerous polling centers of coercive tactics, vote buying, and underage voting. Vote counting was also problematic. When Islah raced ahead in the vote counting in Sanaa, particularly in ruling party strongholds, ruling party officials absented themselves from the counts, thus stalling the process. I was well aware of the phenomenon when I received in the evening a call from the presidency requesting that the United States respond positively to the unusually peaceful election day. In response, I pointed out that we would be guided by the judgment of the NDI delegation of experts, which was alarmed at the ongoing interruption of the count.

Whether it was mounting international pressure or reassuring returns from the hinterland, for whatever reason the ruling party relented. The count in Sanaa resumed, and Islah claimed victory in nearly half of the capital's districts. Their campaign, which featured government corruption, had rung true with many voters. NDI provided a balanced and constructive critique:

These elections . . . were marked by enthusiasm and determination by Yemenis to exercise their right to vote and freely choose their representatives. This deepening sense of democratic entitlement is an important indication of Yemen's progress as an emerging democracy. The elections also demonstrated a number of other positive developments. . . . Nonetheless, the atmosphere of anxiety in the run-up to the elections caused by persistent violence, as well as heavy-handed and coercive measures on election day by elements of the ruling General People's Congress in many polling centers across the country, significant incidents of underage voting and other problems and irregularities are troubling . . . [and] concerted steps to ensure the credibility of this election process and longer-term efforts to ensure the integrity of the political process are essential to further democratic progress.[7]

The State Department spokesman encapsulated the nuanced NDI position as "generally free and fair." We viewed April 27 as a milestone in Yemen's long road to a real, functioning democracy. The Yemenis themselves deserved the lion's share of credit, but NDI had played an important, welcomed, and positive role.

Freedom House, whose assessments had been adopted in the Millennium Challenge process, took note.[8] In December they issued a press release titled: "Global Freedom Gains amid Terror, Uncertainty: Surprising Level of Freedom in Poor Countries Found." Yemen was the only Middle Eastern country to improve its freedom standing: from "not free" to "partly free," "because of increased civic participation in the country's political process."[9]

While the human rights community saw progress, the counterterrorism community saw backsliding. After the escape of the *Cole* suspects, a new concern mounted: infiltration of arms and terrorists from Yemen into Saudi Arabia. The phenomenon was far from novel. Historically, the border between the two countries was disputed and ill defined. Crown Prince Abdullah of Saudi Arabia had made a strategic decision in 2000 to respond to President Saleh's desire to agree on a line in principle and subsequently demarcate it. The Treaty of Jeddah established for the first time a solid basis for stable, positive relations between longtime rivals.

For the tribes that inhabited the border, however, the agreement was unwelcome and ignored. A German colleague recounted her experience in visiting the region.[10] A local sheikh took her for a tour of his domain. After a prolonged drive, he stopped at a vantage point and had her survey the extensive territory where he held sway, then commented they had been traveling in Saudi Arabia for some time.

Yemenis such as Hedi Dulkim, the recently detained al Qaeda operative, had long made a living smuggling. At the vast Talhi suq outside Sa'dah, a visitor could shop among acres of Toyotas, TVs, and all manner of consumer products brought from Saudi Arabia. In the other direction flowed arms, explosives, khat, livestock, and migrant workers.

Saudi imports were not always innocent. The Yemenis complained that terrorism and extremism in this country were largely funded by the largesse of Saudi sheikhs. Washington shared the general concern about Saudi money. My colleagues at Treasury and State were working with their contacts in the kingdom to impose controls on Saudi charities funding al Qaeda operations.

On May 12 in Riyadh, al Qaeda launched the first of many terrorist attacks in Saudi Arabia. Whereas the kingdom had experienced isolated terrorism in the past,[11] al Qaeda was now undertaking a sustained campaign to destabilize the Saudi regime. Washington's long-standing concerns mounted rapidly. Yemen was viewed as an important source of Saudi instability.

A visit by FBI director Mueller in early June provided an opportunity to discuss al Qaeda's exploitation of the porous border, as well as the *Cole* escapees. It was always helpful to have a Washington VIP reinforcing the embassy's insistent message that they must be recaptured. Mueller also usefully expressed Washington's appreciation for Yemen's takedown of the Iraqi Intelligence Service cell.

Director Mueller also announced the establishment of a legal attaché in Embassy Sanaa—and that Steve Gaudin would fill the job. Steve, a veteran of the *Cole* investigation, was an excellent choice. He not only knew the al Qaeda organization intimately, but he also related exceptionally well to the Yemenis. He understood that working in Sanaa would be frustrating but accepted the challenge. Since he needed at least some Arabic, his arrival in Sanaa would unfortunately be delayed. In the meantime, however, he would come in July to administer the first FBI-taught course in Yemen on crime-scene processing.

The July course was indeed a high point in an otherwise disappointing period. Financed by State's antiterrorism money, the FBI trainers were excellent, as were the Yemeni trainees selected by Minister al-Alimi. Familiar with State's antiterrorism program from my days in S/CT, I long felt counterterrorism training would be more effective if given not in the United States, but in the host country where trainers would be forced to deal with the limitations of that environment. The FBI trainers pleasantly surprised us with their ability to communicate and work across the linguistic and cultural divide. They provided the Yemenis not only the skills for crime-scene processing, but cases with the relatively simple tools they needed for the job. I joined the group for their concluding exercise—processing a vehicle rigged to explode at a desert site—and was impressed by the professionalism of all involved and by the seamless cooperation between U.S. and Yemeni partners. At the graduation ceremony, the Yemeni graduates beamed with pride, as each received a diploma and the much-valued crime-scene-processing case. I had rarely seen money better spent. In the years that followed, American specialists would regularly run into these Yemeni graduates, who opened doors for Americans needing to work in Yemen.

During this time, the training by the U.S. and British military of CSF personnel paid an unexpected dividend. Abyan was the poor sister of Aden in the south and long a source of domestic terrorism. The Islamic Army of Aden, also known as the Aden-Abyan Islamic Army, was the most obvious manifestation. It had a history of bombings in the port city of Aden and usually used small improvised explosives to make political points.

In June a Yemeni military medical team undertook a mission into the Jebel Huttat area of Abyan as part of the government's continuing campaign to reach out to deprived areas. We encouraged these efforts. In this instance, some fifty to a hundred members of the Islamic Army of Aden attacked the convoy, killing six and capturing some twelve to twenty others. As in the case of the slaying of the American medical personnel in Jiblah, public opinion swung squarely against the attackers and behind the government. With an unassailable political base, Saleh decided to respond vigorously. The attackers, however, had the advantage of local knowledge of the extremely rugged terrain. The Yemeni military was a blunt instrument whose approach was normally ineffective bombardments. The Yemeni special forces, in which we had invested much training and equipment, were deemed too precious a resource for this mission. Their priority—it was reaffirmed—was regime protection. The right tool proved to be the Interior Ministry's CSF. Colonel Yahya embraced the mission, and his troops performed admirably. Yahya made sure to document their success, and we very much welcomed this evidence that U.S. and U.K. counterterrorism training could be put to good use.

One visitor who appreciated and consistently supported U.S. training of Yemeni counterterrorism forces was the new leader of CENTCOM, Gen. John Abizaid. Mild-mannered and highly intelligent, Abizaid connected immediately with his "troops" in

Yemen, including myself, and with the Yemenis. On an early visit, we took him north of Sanaa to the training range that the U.S. military, led by U.S. Navy SEAL Darby Avant, had sculpted out of sand, shacks, and tires. For next to nothing, the Yemenis could now train in a realistic environment and put their increasing skills on display. General Abizaid praised the effort and won renewed commitment to the enterprise from his own troops and our Yemeni partners. Abizaid connected as well with President Saleh.

In late September Saleh had important news to share in his first meeting with the general: Yemeni security forces had uncovered another cell planning attacks against the American and other embassies. The cell's leader, 'Amr Sharif, had gone about his business in a most amateurish fashion. He had recruited supporters at Al Iman University and set himself up in an apartment to prepare his attacks. Unwisely, he had invited to the apartment a young woman. Sanaa's police took such liaisons seriously. Their vice raid also revealed Sharif's terrorist plans. If Abu Ali represented al Qaeda's "A" team and Fawaz al-Rabi'a its "B" team, we now confronted a "C" team whose links with al Qaeda remained unclear.

Local victories such as the 'Amr Sharif bust did not impress the counterterrorism community in Washington. The White House and most players in CSG were riveted on the Yemeni-Saudi connection, while in DoD and the FBI the *Cole* jailbreak rankled.

State took a more balanced view. In early October Assistant Secretary Bill Burns returned for one of his many visits. Bill had immense responsibilities. He was point man on the Arab-Israeli peace process and, in that capacity, master of the "road map." Iraq also fell within his purview. Nevertheless, he made time for periodic visits to Yemen, with each one significantly advancing our agenda.

In October Bill focused on MEPI, which reflected his penchant to create "a positive agenda" in the Middle East.[12] Having been neglected by State in the traditional funding categories, Embassy Sanaa had seized upon this initiative to obtain the resources we needed in order to address the development side of our security-development equation. There was considerable new democratic growth in Yemen, which was made evident by the recent parliamentary election. We continued to take a disproportionate share of MEPI money and put it to good use. On his October visit, Bill was able to interact with young Yemeni women training counterparts in nongovernmental organizations and the SCER, which was beginning to address the NDI's prescription for improvements in the electoral process.

As always, Saleh was pleased to see Bill who could discuss with him authoritatively both Palestine and Iraq. On the latter, Saleh reiterated his misgivings. On Palestine, Bill's progress with the road map rendered the discussion uncharacteristically positive. Bill also followed up on a very practical note a previous initiative to move the Yemenis to an Article 98 agreement by which Yemen and the United States would handle criminal issues related to their citizens bilaterally and without recourse to the International Criminal Court.[13]

Bill had visited several of our development projects in Sanaa, but our focus was far from the capital. It was time for me to make another trip to Ma'rib. Finally, we had a good reason to do so. The Social Fund had completed a beautiful and functional health center in Sheikh Rabish's village of Madghil, and we were going to inaugurate it. The sheikh naturally wanted to host a lunch for us, but the governor of Ma'rib claimed that prerogative. A hospitality "battle" ensued, until the sheikh graciously conceded. We arrived in Madghil to find the site festooned with pictures of President Saleh and representatives of the governor in charge. We were delighted. I was even more delighted by the crush of villagers, mostly young men with AK-47s slung over their shoulders, who followed us as the clinic's staff conducted a tour of the new facility. The short speeches that followed struck the right notes. We emphasized development as the essential partner of security. Sheikh Rabish proclaimed Madghil a terrorist-free zone. As we prepared to depart, I noticed that the sheikh had exchanged his sash for USAID director Doug Heisler's tie—a spontaneous gesture that summed up for me the partnerships we envisioned throughout Yemen's deprived provinces.

The counterterrorism community in Washington, as far as I could tell, took little note of events such as the dedication of the Madghil clinic. However, from the Afghan-Pakistan border, unhappiness was expressed about security and development trends in Yemen. On October 18, bin Laden spoke out about developments in the Islamic world, including specifically Yemen:

> You young people of Islam everywhere, especially from the neighboring states [of Iraq], and Yemen, you have to wage jihad and show your muscles. . . . There are voices in Iraq, like there were in Palestine, Egypt, Jordan and Yemen and others, that called for peaceful democratic solution to deal with the infidel governments or with the crusader and Jewish invaders, instead of fighting for God. You must be warned against this wrong misleading path that violates God's law.[14]

If only Washington ranked Yemen alongside Egypt, Palestine, and Jordan as a development priority, I thought. We were gaining allies there, however. An important one, USAID director Andrew Natsios, found time to visit in early November and provided his team in Sanaa with a morale boost. Natsios also effectively conveyed a hard and important truth in his meeting with the president. For countries such as Yemen, President Bush's Millennium Challenge represented the best vehicle for obtaining large development assistance. To qualify, however, Yemen would have to undertake significant reforms across a broad spectrum. In development, the United States would help those who helped themselves.

Natsios's tough but positive message on development was to be followed shortly thereafter by an even tougher message on security. FBI director Mueller returned and reflected sharply during his visit the many doubts and misgivings of the Washington counterterrorism community. Uncharacteristically, Director Mueller was not interested in the embassy's assessment of where we stood. He had a fixed agenda: information sharing, the *Cole* escapees, and safeguards in releasing extremists. Interior Minister al-Alimi, whose protection the embassy relied on and whose forces had risen to several challenges—in protecting the embassy against violent demonstrators, arresting Fawaz al-Rabi'a, the Abyan operation, the 'Amr Sharif cell—offered the guest an *iftar* as it was Ramadan and President Saleh required time to break his fast.[15] Following advice from his party, Mueller refused to attend, thereby insulting his host.

The meeting with Saleh was therefore uncomfortable, but it gave me an opportunity to draw his attention to reports that al Qaeda operative Abu Assem was in Sanaa and to urge Yemeni action. Significantly, Saleh's staff did not dispute the reports. I hoped that we had pointed the Yemenis toward a helpful step.

Since Mueller's staff was rushing him on to his next stop, we proceeded immediately to the airport. For the only time during my service in Sanaa, I vented. I recognized that Washington was unsatisfied with the Yemeni government's performance on a number of counts. I too was unsatisfied. That said, we needed to acknowledge where progress had been made, particularly in al-Alimi's Interior Ministry, and we needed to recognize our shortcomings. For one, I still did not have my permanent legal attaché five months after we had announced an appointment with fanfare in Aden.

It hurt. Among my American colleagues, there were none I respected more than Bob Mueller. Among our Yemeni partners, none more than the interior minister. A natural connection had been missed altogether. Unlike Foreign Minister al-Qirby, al-

Alimi spoke next to no English, so they could not relate directly. Mueller was also looking beyond al-Alimi to President Saleh, an approach that correctly recognized Saleh as the ultimate decision maker but undervalued al-Alimi's critical role in both shaping and implementing those decisions. Had the FBI had its own person with adequate Arabic working day in and day out with the Interior Ministry, I believe the director would have then had a more balanced picture. As it was, I was sure that the FBI director would soon be reporting and reporting unfavorably on his meeting in Sanaa with our Yemeni "partner."

CHAPTER TEN

BACK ON TRACK

B ob Mueller's visit had been difficult. We had not been diplomatic in the naïve
sense of the word. Fortunately, President Saleh was a blunt speaker who prid-
ed himself on talking straight to the superpower. Other leaders in the Middle
East, he repeatedly told American visitors, will tell you what you want to hear; I, on
the other hand, will tell you what you need to hear. The flip side was that Saleh did not
generally take offense when spoken to bluntly by someone he respected, and he certainly respected Mueller. In the end, counterterrorism was better served by directness
from visitors rather than circumlocution that would leave Saleh thinking all was well.

The first proof came at the end of July when the Yemeni security forces surround-
ed Abu Assem in his Sanaa location, and he surrendered. He had come to Sanaa for his
wedding, which in al Qaeda code often designated a terrorist attack. But in this case, it
was a real wedding. (Sometimes, as Freud observed, a cigar is just a cigar.) He had done
so furtively and had exposed himself for only brief periods, but they were nevertheless
sufficient to compromise his location. Most of his work, in the end, had been directed
at raising funds in Saudi Arabia to support families of deceased mujahideen. Consid-
ering the circumstances of his capture, it seemed much had changed since al Qaeda's
heyday when its leaders enjoyed safe havens in the remote provinces and could plan in
security their attacks on such targets as the USS *Cole* and our embassy. In the conduct
of counterterrorism, things too had changed. The operation against Abu Assem was a
Yemeni one, and it would be the model for the future.

President Saleh understandably expected his action to catch Washington's attention. Washington, however, remained skeptical. Would the Yemenis sustain their cam-

paign? Would Abu Assem's knowledge be tapped and exploited? Would he remain in jail or, like the *Cole* suspects, escape? Wait and see was the prevailing mood.

President Saleh found this frustrating. When my predecessor, Ambassador Bodine, arrived on a visit in mid-December to wrap up the negotiations on the Article 98 accord, which she had managed deftly throughout, Saleh took advantage of their re-union to vent his frustration. "I never hear 'thank you,'" he complained. Ambassa-dor Bodine gallantly rose in defense. She compared the current U.S. engagement in Yemen—economic assistance, MEPI projects, coast guard boats, training, equipping security forces—with what had been possible in her time. Progress, she argued, was quite remarkable.

Meanwhile, Saleh and his government were pursuing a new vocation: democracy. The parliamentary election in March had gone surprisingly well, and the world had noticed. Just as significant were the post-election politics. The newly elected parlia-mentarians organized themselves in a different spirit than their predecessors. With international recognition, they displayed greater confidence and more independence. Committee assignments were hotly contested, especially those committees that dealt with foreign affairs and Yemen's oil and gas wealth. Ministers found themselves begin-ning to be held accountable. "Young Turks" looked over their shoulder at the presiden-cy to see if their democratic maneuvers were approaching red lines, but the president stayed his hand.

The Europeans wanted to engage. NDI's courageous decision to proceed with monitoring the parliamentary election in April despite the ongoing conflict in Iraq demonstrated that the EU had been mistaken in holding back its own monitors. Now the EU proposed a grand democracy conference in Sanaa in January 2004 to look forward.

There was an ulterior motive, however, that gave us pause. The conference was also intended to promote the International Criminal Court, which the United States was boycotting. My European colleagues were also lobbying against special arrange-ments—the Article 98 agreements—that we had just concluded with Yemen. We checked with the State Department and found little relish for such a meeting.

In this instance, I tended to agree. I was not bothered so much by the court theme, which we had finessed with Ambassador Bodine's effort, but was suspicious of large, expensive public conferences. They tended to produce rhetorical support for democracy but little practical action. Over the previous two years, I had watched the progress of democracy in Yemen. It had been the day-in, day-out efforts of the SCER and its international supporters, and, most importantly, the Yemeni people—partisans, poll watchers, and voters—who had produced significant progress. There was no substitute, in my view, for that level of engagement. The Europeans wanted a curtain call but had missed the rehearsals and the performance.

I was too harsh. My stance was too parochial. The Middle East was approaching a moment when the issue of democracy was moving from the periphery to the center. The vast entourage gathered in Sanaa helped such enlightened Yemeni figures as Foreign Minister al-Qirby to produce a statement, subsequentlly called the Sanaa Declaration, that was remarkably progressive.[1]

The foreign minister and I were soon to gauge more truly the importance of the declaration that he was instrumental in producing. To express our respect for the foreign minister's overall diplomacy, we decided that Secretary Powell should meet with al-Qirby. In late January, I was back in Washington accompanying the foreign minister on his rounds. As usual, he was urbane and effective in his meetings.

The surprise came at the meeting with Deputy Adviser for National Security Stephen Hadley and Senior Director for the Middle East Elliot Abrams. Unlike any other White House meeting that I had attended involving Yemen, this one did not begin with terrorism. Rather, NSC officials wanted to discuss the Sanaa Declaration and democracy in the Middle East. Al-Qirby was delighted to do so. From the Yemeni experience, both practical and theoretical, there was much to say, and al-Qirby did it eloquently.

For a change, there was also good news on the assistance front. While State continued to underperform, in my view, on the main assistance programs, Assistant Secretary for Economic and Business Affairs Tony Wayne, who had worked in the Secretary's counterterrorism office early in his career, helped produce from the U.S. Department of Agriculture a generous allocation for Yemen of the agricultural surplus resources.[2] Both the foreign minister and I could return to Sanaa with positive news.

The Yemen experience also began to gain attention in the region. The Joint Task Force for the Horn of Africa, whose headquarters was located in Djibouti, sponsored a meeting of regional ambassadors in mid-February. They reached across the Bab al-Mandab, the strait that separated Yemen from Africa, and I was the only ambassador included from the Near East bureau. General Abizaid provided an overview from the command. He radiated common sense, confidence, and humility. We could ask for no better partner.

On the second day, I was asked to present on the Yemeni experience and sketched out for my colleagues the path we had followed. I emphasized not the dramatic head-lines such as the elimination of Abu Ali, but the longer, ultimately more productive slog in training the Yemeni security forces, particularly Interior Ministry forces, that was now producing arrests. General Abizaid graciously posited the Yemeni experience as a model for the region.

Back in Sanaa the following week after an unanticipated layover in Eritrea because of a broken airplane, I experienced another dip in the roller coaster of U.S.-Yemeni relations. The terrorist-financing folks in Washington had long identified Sheikh Ab-dulmajid Zindani, head of Al Iman University and a leader of the Islah Party, as a supporter of terrorism. I had no doubts that Al Iman was a focal point for extremist thinking in Yemen. Indeed, early in my tenure, numerous Yemeni officials had voiced their wish that funding to Al Iman from Saudi Arabia and other Gulf states be inter-rupted. On that basis, we had made démarches to Gulf governments in an effort to discourage direct funding for Al Iman. Now the U.S. effort would take an overt and, for the Yemenis, a politically problematic form.

The U.S. designation of Zindani as a supporter of terrorism raised howls of pro-test from the opposition and strong negative comments from the government. I di-rected attention to Al Iman and the fact that it had served as a venue for both the 'Amr Sharif cell members and Ali Jarallah, the assassin of Yemeni Socialist Party leader Jarallah Omar. As with Sheikh al-Moayad, my arguments found little overt support. Still, the relatively restrained nature of the government's response suggested that it was not entirely unhappy to have an Islah notable on the defensive.

Meanwhile, the Yemeni security forces were making gains in continued efforts against the remaining al Qaeda organization. When the Predator struck, one of Abu Ali's entourage, Ra'uf Nassib, had managed to walk away. We had thought he had ex-pired somewhere in the desert, but his body was never found. Now, after more than a year, Nassib was arrested. More importantly, Interior Minister al-Alimi was honoring his commitment to pursue the *Cole* escapees. One of the small fry, Mohamed al-Ahdal, had been arrested on September 25, 2003. Now, in March 2004, a second one, Mo-hamed Darameh, was picked up. Finally, on March 18, the principals, Jamal al-Badawi and Fahd al-Quso, were arrested. The major blot on Yemen's counterterrorism record and source of Washington's skepticism about Yemen's continuing commitment was expunged. This time the American thanks came not belatedly and orally from the ambassador, but promptly in writing from Bob Mueller in the FBI. It was well received. The prisoners this time were moved to a PSO facility in Sanaa, and their trial was put on a fast track. Lessons had been learned.

Just as the Yemenis had put their counterterrorism efforts into a higher gear, so had we geared up our development efforts. The reopening of our USAID mission in Sanaa had a substantial public diplomacy impact. Even absent economic development funds, USAID's renewed presence recalled a happier time in the relationship and stood as a promise for better times ahead. Doug Heisler, our new USAID director, realized that the U.S. embassy in Sanaa could not responsibly administer millions in assistance without enhancing its own capacity. He set out to do so by first winning the trust and loyalty of the staff that had already been putting forth a surprisingly effective, improvised assistance effort. Then, for modest salaries, he hired several Yemenis with advanced degrees, native Arabic, and excellent connections back to the Yemeni government and society. Together with Ahmed Sufan's thin but competent staff in the Ministry of International Cooperation and Planning, the Social Fund, and the Public Works Project, the development program moved forward smartly.

When we returned to Ma'rib in late January, this progress was evident. Our efforts in the health field had previously been symbolized by the new health center in Madghil, which was performing beyond our expectations. The staff of a doctor, a nurse, and a pharmacist was treating an average of fifty patients a day who were virtually all making some payment for their services. The facility remained in good condition with its staff planning sensible expansion of services.

Now in late January, the massive regional hospital was also nearing completion. I met with some of the young people from Ma'rib who would staff the facility and whose training in Sanaa we were financing. They spoke of their challenge. Less prepared than their counterparts from elsewhere in Yemen, they were nevertheless determined to make the grade and return to jobs providing a vital service in Ma'rib. We also witnessed the first graduation of female extension agents who, we hoped, could bring useful information and techniques to the numerous shepherdesses who controlled Ma'rib's animal wealth.

We re-examined ongoing archaeology projects and discussed the potential for tourism, and visited the expansive site designated for the Ma'rib museum. I was convinced that Ma'rib would be a successful showcase for Yemeni-U.S. development cooperation. It was time to push further. I asked my staff to prepare a development trip to an even more remote, wilder province: Al Jawf.

We had not neglected the security side of the equation. In Ma'rib U.S. Marines and Special Forces had responded to the Yemeni request to build from scratch special forces units to bring government control finally to this far-flung part of Yemen. The recruits were tough local youths. They had never worn boots, but they had carried AK-47s since their early teens. The training effort was often frustrating. We continued to miss dearly a Yemeni noncommissioned officer grade that could provide continuity and leadership. But, with CENTCOM's support, the effort continued.

Meanwhile, Capt. Bob Innis pulled rabbit after rabbit from his hat in making the Yemeni Coast Guard a reality. Tough-minded, Bob forced much of the work and most of the decisions back on his Yemeni colleagues. Under Interior Minister al-Alimi, they were highly motivated and effective within the limits of their authority. Bob had secured for them prime training spots in U.S. Coast Guard programs, and they had rewarded his efforts by finishing among the top of the foreign students enrolled. Bob had also brought out to Aden training teams to continue training in the real, often deprived environment of Yemen. As he helped the Yemenis build an esprit de corps, he simultaneously helped them develop an infrastructure to support their force. The true challenge was not in procuring the end items (the boats) but rather the workshops, lifts, training facilities, and trained personnel to maintain and use them effectively.[3] Bob helped the Yemenis identify Camp Nasser, an underused facility next to Aden International Airport, to serve as the coast guard's main training camp. They also located and acquired a spectacular site for the coast guard headquarters in the center of Aden Port. Bob proposed that unlike any other security establishment in Yemen, it be accessible to ordinary Yemenis who could better appreciate and support the coast guard's services.

On April 7, 2004, the commissioning of the first seven boats from the United States took place.[4] The ceremony was run impressively by the coast guard's leadership. Aden's new governor, Yahya Al-Shuabi, attended as did Brig. Gen. Mastin Robeson from CENTCOM's Horn of Africa Task Force. The speeches were relatively short. Then we boarded for a tour of Aden's harbor, knowing those responsible for the attack on the *Cole* were dead or in custody. Aden's water was now patrolled by U.S.-supplied and -trained forces deeply committed to preventing any recurrence of the attack. It appeared to me that al Qaeda's attack on the *Cole* on October 12, 1999, had had for that organization unintended and very negative consequences.

With the *Cole* escapees recaptured, the Yemeni government lost no time in moving their case to trial. In fact, two trials proceeded in rapid succession. The first group included Fawaz al-Rabi'a and the members of his cell, and the Walid al-Shaibah cell. They had much to answer for: the bombing of PSO locations in the spring of 2002, the attack on the M/V *Limburg* in October of that year, the attack on the Hunt Oil helicopter in November, plots to attack the American and other embassies, and finally the assassination plot against me. This trial was to be followed by that of Jamal al-Badawi, Fahd al-Quso, and associates for the *Cole* attack.

Fortunately, Steve Gaudin, our legal attaché, was by then finally in place and able to interface with the office of Yemen's prosecutor general, equivalent to the United States's attorney general. Steve had the great additional benefit of access to the FBI's lead investigator, who brought not only his encyclopedic knowledge of the case, but volumes of related facts and evidence that the FBI had prepared to support a prosecution of defendants in U.S. courts.

Throughout the trials, the defendants expressed defiance. They and their supporters did their maximum to intimidate the prosecution and the FBI personnel present. Our representatives were identified by the defendants with implied threats, as they attended the proceedings that, initially at least, resembled a circus. Gradually, however, the Yemeni authorities took hold of the situation, reconfigured the courtroom, and began to impose order.

In the court proceedings, the magnitude of the terrorist plots that we had only vaguely perceived came into focus. In retrospect, our security measures to harden the embassy and my motorcade had proven thoroughly justified and effective in complicating the planning and execution of the plots. The terrorists were also revealed as intelligent and resourceful but far, far from perfect in their planning and execution. They had made mistakes, most notably the misfired missile in August 2002. The Yemeni-U.S. partners in counterterrorism had made them pay for those mistakes.

After my departure on August 28, the Sanaa Court convicted fourteen al Qaeda members for the attack on the M/V *Limburg*, the murder of a security officer associated with the attack on the Hunt Oil helicopter, the bombing plots in Sanaa, and the plot to kill me. Two defendants were sentenced to death, one in absentia. The other defendants were sentenced to prison for periods from three to ten years.[5] Also, on September 10, the same court convicted five al Qaeda members for the attack on the *Cole*. The two ringleaders, Abd al-Rahim al-Nashiri and Jamal al-Badawi, subsequently received death sentences, al-Nashiri in absentia. Three others were sentenced to prison from five to ten years.[6] In both cases, both the prosecution and defense appealed.[7]

As justice was being served in Yemeni courts, a rough justice was being served in the court of Yemeni public opinion. We had made efforts in development no less than in security but had received little recognition. Privately with President Saleh, my predecessor had pointed out the distance traveled. We needed public recognition of that effort.

I asked my staff to begin documenting U.S. assistance to Yemen for the period 2001–4 to coincide roughly with President Saleh and President Bush's strategic agreement in the Oval Office in November 2001. Led by a talented entry-level Foreign Service officer, Melisa Doherty, they produced a concise PowerPoint presentation. Despite being largely denied the standard tools of security and development assistance, particularly economic support funds and foreign military funding, we had cobbled together a program of nearly $150 million, which was roughly equaled in assistance for which we could not take public credit. The specifics were impressive:

- approximately $41.1 million for education and culture, including 200 schools and 200,000 school desks (each bearing the qamariya logo identifying it as a gift of the United States), and $2 million for women's literacy and computers for 20 schools in Sanaa, Aden, and other governorates
- $5.7 million to send 175 Yemenis, from high school to the post-doctorate level, to the United States for further education
- $27 million for health care, including building, renovating, or equipping 40 health facilities, training 256 health staff, and aiding both local councils and the Ministry of Health in planning and reform
- $6 million to promote democracy and human rights, including electoral activity, nongovernment organizations, local councils, and women's political activity
- $56 million in infrastructure, agriculture, and economic development, including roads, the Sa'ilah project in central Sanaa,[8] water, and agriculture

Of the above, approximately $10 million had gone to Ma'rib in forty-eight projects that covered the spectrum.

On the security side, we could point to TIP funded at $15 million to provide facilities, computers, and related equipment at every Yemeni airport, seaport, and land border crossing. A formidable electronic net had been spread across one of al Qaeda's preferred transit countries. We calculated $8.5 million in assistance to stand up the Yemeni Coast Guard, an effort that included base and building acquisitions, recruiting six hundred personnel, training thirty in navigation and port security, English language training, advanced training in the United States, and the refurbishing and delivery of the initial eight patrol boats.

With Under Secretary John Bolton's support, the de-mining program remained strong and had received $750,000 for vehicles, ambulances, forklifts, communications, and other equipment.

Finally, a debt-forgiveness package, agreed in July 2002, had reduced Yemen's official debt by $75 million.

Minister Sufan agreed with my argument that the Yemeni people needed to know and appreciate how much had been done, particularly by virtue of USDA's 416b program, which had served us so well when virtually no other funds were at hand. He assigned Nabil Shaiban, a key staff member who moonlighted as an English newscaster on Yemen TV, to work with the embassy. Nabil was an inspired choice. He not only knew the details of U.S. assistance intimately, but he had also been to the United States in his media capacity to study documentary production. His resulting program on the 416b assistance aired on Yemen TV.

Since the *Cole* attack in 2000, Yemen's "vocation" had largely been counterterrorism in the eyes of Americans. In the aftermath of 9/11, that calling from Washington had intensified. On the ground in Sanaa, we had consciously chosen to pursue the objective of eradicating al Qaeda and denying it Yemeni operating space through a broad strategy of promoting development, including democracy and human rights. During Foreign Minister al-Qirby's trip to Washington, we had heard the first voices in the Bush administration linking democracy in Yemen and the Middle East generally to U.S. strategic interests. Now in the spring of 2004, I received a call from NSC's Elliot Abrams with a surprising proposal: would President Saleh accept an invitation from President Bush to join the leaders of the industrialized countries, the G-8, in Sea Island, Georgia, to discuss democracy in the Middle East?

Yemen and President Saleh had rarely been on Washington's A-list for any purpose. Generally, that status for Arab leaders was reserved for those who had made peace with Israel or controlled vast oil reserves. But the times they were a-changin', and Yemen's parliamentary elections and the Sanaa Declaration had put Yemen in select company for the first time.

Knowing Saleh would be interested in the company he might be keeping, I asked about other invitees. Several other Arab heads of state were likely to attend but not President Hosni Mubarak of Egypt or King Abdullah of Saudi Arabia. Most significantly, Israeli prime minister Ariel Sharon was not going to be invited, so there was no question of a surreptitious attempt to build bridges between Israel and the Arab world.

I took two actions. First, I wanted to ensure that Assistant Secretary Bill Burns in State was aware of NSC's initiative. Ever since John Kelly as ambassador in Lebanon became entangled in Oliver North's Iran-Contra affair, the president has instructed U.S. ambassadors in writing that their guidance normally come via the secretary of state. In this instance, I had no reason to believe that NSC, on which I had served, was acting improperly, but prudence dictated that State be kept in the loop.

Relatively soon I received confirmation and some elaboration of the G-8 proposal from the Near East bureau. On that basis, I took the matter to Presidential Adviser al-Iryani for an unofficial but authoritative reaction from the president prior to a formal invitation. While al-Iryani sought that, Foreign Minister al-Qirby asked to see me. He had received word via Ambassador al-Hajri in Washington of the White House initiative. What did I know? Respecting al-Qirby greatly, I confirmed Ambassador al-Hajri's report and noted that al-Iryani had already undertaken to get President Saleh's reaction. At this informal stage, I explained, I thought it best not to involve the Foreign Ministry's bureaucracy lest the proposal leak, creating unnecessary pressure and possible embarrassment. Unlike the majority of foreign ministers I had known, al-Qirby's ego was not inflated, and he handled the affair matter of factly. Again, how fortunate I was in my Yemeni partner.

Word came back from the palace: "yes" with the proviso that the Israeli prime minister was not to attend. I was reasonably confident that this was not an issue given the list of potential attendees.

Thus, on June 9, 2004, Saleh was in Washington for the second time in my tenure as ambassador. It had been just over two and a half years since that meeting in the Oval Office when President Bush, still coping with the aftermath of 9/11, and President Saleh made their personal and eventually effective pact to rid Yemen of al Qaeda terrorism.

This time, Saleh would not visit the Oval Office. His session with President Bush would take place at Sea Island in a few days' time. Otherwise, Saleh's Washington schedule was a dream. Usually, visiting leaders met three or four of the administration's top officials. Saleh would see them all: Vice President Cheney, Secretary Powell, Secretary Rumsfeld, CIA director Tenet, and FBI director Mueller. And, most appropriately, given the essential role that agricultural funding played in our broad counterterrorism strategy, U.S. secretary of agriculture Ann Veneman.

Saleh's last meeting with a senior U.S. official had been the previous November when Bob Mueller had visited abruptly with a harsh message. It had been bitter medicine for our counterterrorism relationship but arguably an effective tonic. To everyone's satisfaction, this time the FBI director could begin by reiterating thanks for the recapture of the *Cole* suspects, now defendants in the Yemeni legal proceedings. In a gracious nod to the departing ambassador, Saleh suggested that Hull might just as well be left in Sanaa "if you don't need him elsewhere."

With Mueller, there was respect. With Tenet, I thought I perceived affection. Maybe it was only my imagination, but he had just announced his resignation, and Saleh began their meeting "rejecting it"—as if he were in Yemen dealing with a reluctant but valued warrior. Tenet pronounced himself "tired" and ready to move on. Saleh showered praise. "You have met all challenges . . . principled . . . courageous," and finally, "We were surprised by your decision."

"Sometimes," the director said simply, "it is good to surprise people."

Did he mean specifically Abu Ali and his associates? No matter. It fit.

The director then got to his message for the meeting. The war on terror would last long, into the next generation. The essential factor for partnerships to prosper was "consistency." All along there had been openings in Yemen—al Qaeda operatives caught in the act—who could provide timely information to prevent terrorist acts. That was the information he needed to acquire and to share.

Tenet's days as director were numbered to thirty; he wanted to leave in place a strong U.S.-Yemeni relationship. There were issues, small in comparison to what had been accomplished, that needed attention to ensure that legacy. For its part, the United States had invested a significant sum to support Yemen's counterterrorism efforts. It could do better. Both sides needed to act further. But there was also a time for thanks, and now was the time to thank him for his kindness, friendship, and leadership.

The Department of Agriculture does not spring to mind as a locus of foreign policy, much less counterterrorism. Yet, without USDA, the embassy's ambitious reach into al Qaeda's sanctuaries such as Ma'rib would have been nice theory and little practice. Yemen and my embassy owed a great debt to American farmers and the Washington establishment that protected them.[9]

Not standing on protocol, Saleh called at the Department of Agriculture to meet and thank Secretary Veneman. He breezed through his talking points while fiddling with a Swiss Army pocketknife. Secretary Veneman was gracious in her response, thanking Saleh for Yemen's counterterrorism assistance and noting that USDA had provided $200 million in food aid to Yemen over the past five years. Then, she announced, a further $36 million in wheat flour and non-fat dry milk. She also proposed $10 million in a facilities guarantee program. Saleh responded with enthusiasm, envisioning silos and storage facilities throughout Yemen. He wanted U.S. assistance to take forms visible to the Yemeni people in order to enhance friendship. The lovefest concluded. I thanked the secretary's staff on the way out. Her senior assistant acknowledged my gratitude but then cautioned against unrealistic expectations. Now on budget, 416b confronted inexorable pressures. Lean years lay ahead.

The Pentagon was Saleh's next stop. In 2001 his meeting with Secretary Rumsfeld had been his most contentious, clouded by the misunderstanding on the *Cole* trial and Rumsfeld's generally faulty meeting preparation. Three and a half years later, both were able to relax and mark the progress. Rumsfeld recalled his first meeting with Saleh in 1984 as the Middle East envoy of President Reagan, for whom the Pentagon's flags were now flying at half mast. Saleh, who would extend his stay to attend the state funeral, called the former president "a great man." Rumsfeld cited Reagan's bold, visionary leadership and unfailing good humor.

Turning to counterterrorism, Saleh ran down the list of Yemen's accomplishments. Rumsfeld appreciated what he termed "the impressive heartening improvement in our relations" over the past two and a half years. Then the conversation turned to future cooperation.

The Pentagon meeting concluded, Saleh's motorcade sped toward the White House. There had been no competition for the seat next to Yemen's mercurial president. Only Abdulkarim al-Iryani appeared to be comfortable in the great man's presence, so he took it. That left one car for the foreign minister, Ambassador al-Hajri, State Department interpreter Gamal Helal, a few other Yemeni staffers, and me. Fortunately, the trip across the Potomac took almost no time with our security escort. As a result, we arrived at the West Wing slightly early. As we browsed the painting of *Washington Crossing the Delaware* in the reception room, I tried to keep the president occupied, but his frequent looks at his wristwatch evinced impatience. That evaporated, however, when we were finally shown into Cheney's modest office.

Saleh apologized for being early. The vice president welcomed Saleh and thanked him for the hospitality shown during his brief visit to Sanaa. President Bush was looking forward to seeing him with the G-8. The ensuing conversation focused on terrorism and political reform in the Middle East.

Saleh's last meeting before departing for the heady company of Sea Island was with Secretary Powell. Their meeting in the aftermath of 9/11 had qualified as a diplomatic disaster. Its silver lining then had been that Saleh seemed to have realized how badly he had failed to relate to Washington's concerns and consequently focused all the more for his crucial meeting with the president, which would lay the foundation for the next two and a half years of ultimately effective counterterrorism. On this occasion, Saleh did not miss his opportunity with the secretary. In the context of the administration's new Greater Middle East Initiative, Saleh argued that Yemen had been engaged in its reforms for fourteen years. More could be done if there would be more economic support. Standard arguments perhaps, but the relatively successful parliamentary elections and subsequent Sanaa Declaration lent significant credibility to his words.

Saleh pleaded with Powell for the United States to tackle peace between Israel and Arabs with the same determination that it had had in Bosnia. The road map was good but needed vigorous implementation. Powell pointed to Assistant Secretary Bill Burns, the author of the road map. The United States would continue efforts with Sharon— Gaza and beyond. Palestinian leader Yasser Arafat needed to allow more cooperation, especially on security.

Finally, Saleh noted Yemen's many counterterrorism achievements since 9/11 and the continuing efforts discussed in his excellent meetings around Washington. More expressions of gratitude would be welcome. "Thanks," Powell said, and he meant it.

Sea Island had limited participation, and American ambassadors did not make the cut. Interpreters were essential, however, so Gamal Helal was on hand and provided a subsequent readout. Saleh was resplendent in traditional Yemeni dress, including a ceremonial jambiyya, which President Bush admired. Saleh made a relatively long— ten-minute—presentation at lunch, which was well received by President Bush and the other G-8 leaders.

Saleh's trip to Washington for the G-8 summit was the second "bookend" for my tour in Yemen. It provided me, as ambassador, an authoritative Washington perspective from all major Washington players. Clearly, dramatic progress had been made. The Oval Office deal struck in November 2001 had been substantially kept. Saleh justifiably pointed to the elimination of al Qaeda's first, second, and third tiers in Yemen. For its part, the United States had provided effective support to build up Yemeni security forces, help with economic development, and assistance in promoting Yemen's own democracy.

A certain scratchiness persisted in the relationship, however. Bare-knuckled diplomacy continued to be employed by both sides to get what they wanted. As a professional diplomat accustomed to the niceties of Middle East indirection and State Department politesse, I could never feel totally comfortable. More understanding of, and consideration for, each other would not hurt, it seemed to me. But on both sides the leaders and many of their lieutenants were unvarnished originals. They understood each other well enough. And since there were always the diplomats from both sides to absorb the shocks, the relationship remained on the rails.

Back in Sanaa, only two months remained in my tenure. Two months were just enough to accommodate two long-awaited trips. After much preparation and a false start, my embassy team was finally ready to launch us into Al Jawf, Yemen's most remote area bordering Saudi Arabia. In the newly elected parliamentarian, Feisal Abu Ras, we had in the north an ideal partner.

Feisal was equal parts Yemeni sheikh and U.S.-educated diplomat. He perfectly bridged the gap between the two cultures and was inexhaustible in ideas for bringing progress and stability to Al Jawf. Like many Yemenis a student of history, he had found in Al Jawf's long, long tribal traditions, a golden age when the region had prospered from trade because its tribes had strictly secured the routes of that trade. Prosperity could return to Al Jawf, he argued, if its tribes returned to securing their land.

By now the embassy team was well practiced at extending development projects into remote areas. Several scouting efforts, which included our good partners from the Social Fund and the Public Works Project, had identified a dozen health projects worthy of support. In almost all cases, Ahmed Attieg and Shaif al-Hamdany had assessed the stone structures to be sound. Our funds would be directed at renovations, equipping, and most significantly training people from the area who live in decent quarters at the centers to provide services. We had seen this model work in Madghil and wanted to replicate it now in Al Jawf.

The embassy convoy that left early on June 21 included a robust media component, including Yemeni TV and journalists from major government and nongovernment newspapers. Amal accompanied me as she was keen on seeing Al Jawf's archaeological treasures and was a great fan of Feisal. USAID chief Doug Heisler also joined for the first day. All security and most of the substantive program had been done by the embassy's exceptionally competent Foreign Service nationals.

We took the road to Ma'rib but midway turned north to Al Hazm. By late morning we arrived, and the governor and his wife welcomed us as gracious hosts. His newly completed residence accommodated us most comfortably.[10] We spoke long and in some detail about his hopes for developing Al Jawf. He welcomed our efforts on health but pushed for an agricultural program to tap the vast region's potential. With experience in Ma'rib and continuing 416b funds, at least for a year or so, I could promise to help. I asked about security. Smiling, he told me he had his own concerns when it came to protecting the American ambassador. So, he had sent agents out in advance to consult with the tribal chiefs whose areas we would visit. One particularly rough individual received a hard look and frank talk. "Don't worry," the chief replied when asked if the ambassador would be treated well. "We understand that we will get much more from the Americans if we behave than if we threaten." It was a simple calculus but one I was pleased to find in Yemen's wildest east.

Long, long hours on the road followed far beyond the governorate's capital of Al Hazm. Ahmed and Shaif wanted to make sure I understood how vast and desolate Al Jawf was. By the time we finally returned to the governor's hospitality, we were ready to sit down with our media friends and speak with some credibility based on what we had seen and what we had already programmed to do. I was upbeat as were the governor and the Yemeni officials from the Social Fund and the Public Works Project. After the formal bit, I suggested that the journalists sit with us and just talk about what we were seeing. Not accustomed to "backgrounders" or being treated as professionals, the reporters welcomed the opportunity.

Their questions were good ones. Among the best: "Why was the American ambassador so interested in Yemeni tribes and tribal areas like Ma'rib and now Al Jawf?" Implicit in the question was concern that, as with Saudi Arabia previously, the United States somehow wanted to build an independent power base in Yemen's tribal north.

I replied that President Saleh had drawn my attention to Yemen's deprived areas shortly after my arrival in Sanaa in 2001. He had correctly, in my view, pointed out that their development was important to Yemen's political well-being. I had adopted that agenda and done what I could, with the full knowledge of, and in full cooperation with, Yemen's government. Our purpose was to help Yemen's government help the citizens of these regions.

As for the tribes, I felt they played a positive role in Yemen. They provided identity and social support. Neither the Yemeni government nor the United States looked upon them as the enemy. Sheikh Abdullah al-Ahmar's admonition that "all Yemenis are tribesmen, and all tribesmen are Yemeni" had captured the essence of the matter for me.

Our second day in Al Jawf was longer than the first. By now, all the other Americans except Amal and me had returned to Sanaa. We went about our visits, which culminated in Feisal's stronghold of Barat al-Inan. Only once—during a visit to a remote health center—did a resident accost us and berate American policy. In a small structure and under the press of scores of AK-47–armed tribesmen, my security chief, Mahmoud, deftly maneuvered us into a holding room while the local sheikhs remonstrated with the protester and escorted him away.

Once we reached Feisal's territory, we felt ourselves truly at home. We enjoyed his company and his hospitality immensely. Seeing Al Jawf through his visionary eyes, we were pleased that our days in Yemen were just enough to allow the trip. My trip to Al Jawf was widely reported on Yemeni TV and in the print media. For those uncomfortable with the American ambassador's travels, there would be no respite.

If Al Jawf represented promise, then Ma'rib was fulfillment. With a scarce four days left in my tenure as ambassador, I made my final trip there on July 17, 2004. Again Amal accompanied, and together we marked two milestones. First, we dedicated the site of the Ma'rib museum, a project now in the hands of the Social Fund. Second, we welcomed the first significant delivery of equipment to the regional hospital, which had become a symbol of American commitment to improving lives in the Ma'rib region.

As I paid my farewell calls, I enjoyed providing impressions of Al Jawf and Ma'rib to the senior Yemeni officials with whom I was saying good-bye. The opposition media was incensed by the image of the American ambassador traveling in Yemen's remote areas. Constantly decrying my "violation" of diplomatic protocol, they ignored the simple fact that the travel, the contacts, and the projects were openly done—the Yemeni journalists were our witnesses—and fully coordinated with local and national authorities.

President Saleh made no such complaints. He accorded me the honor of a farewell meeting. The glow of Sea Island and his trip to Washington had not yet dissipated. He thanked me for my service and presented a medal commemorating Yemeni independence as a token of that appreciation. In turn, I thanked him for our partnership and congratulated him on its accomplishments. I had violated protocol on my first meeting as ambassador by raising specific threats and urging practical steps. In fact, I had not been particularly careful in observing protocol thereafter. In a sense, the formal diplomacy of a European capital or a Middle Eastern court never really applied in Sanaa. Desperate times had occasionally called for desperate measures. Now, for the first and only time, I asked nothing of the president and he asked nothing of me.

AFTERWORD

One battle does not make a war—particularly the "long war" against al Qaeda, which began for most Americans on 9/11. Al Qaeda in Yemen learned from its setbacks between 2001 and 2004 and reconstituted itself so as to threaten not only Yemeni and U.S. interests there, but also the region and, on Christmas Day 2009, the U.S. homeland. Can we identify the turning points? How has Al Qaeda in the Arabian Peninsula come back? What lessons should be learned in order to deny a safe haven for al Qaeda in Yemen?

By the summer of 2004, the al Qaeda network in Yemen had ceased to function. Its leadership had been either killed or captured, with disorganized remnants engaged in amateurish plots.[1] A potent organization that had nearly sunk a U.S. warship was virtually defunct. The Yemeni government, particularly CSF, was making good use of training and equipment and had seized the initiative. American and international support was still required, but it was restricted to an indirect role in areas such as intelligence, equipment, and training. The Yemeni Coast Guard was stood up and promising, and the program to monitor Yemen's entry and exit points—TIP—was up and running.

The American embassy's development program was increasingly professional. While still underfunded, it had proven models of success, particularly in the Madghil clinic, and had pushed well beyond Ma'rib in identifying similar projects in Al Jawf and Shabwah. As American ambassador, I could travel in Yemen's most remote areas without any American security personnel. The embassy's Yemeni bodyguards, Interior Ministry escort, and, most importantly, protection from the tribes, whose well-being

111

we served, provided all the needed security even though I had been the specific target of an al Qaeda assassination plot.

Great challenges remained. Yemen's political development had made substantial progress with the parliamentary elections of 2003, which were judged by the international community to be generally free and fair. The new Parliament continued to include active opposition parties as well as a younger, more assertive generation of the ruling party. Nevertheless, disproportionate political power continued to reside in the presidency, and the central government was widely perceived as corrupt with its accounts hidden, most notably oil and later gas revenues. Government ministries failed to provide such essential services as health and education in many parts of the country. Macro-economic reform remained largely unaddressed. Yemen continued to exhaust its resources of oil and water, while its reputation for corruption discouraged foreign investment and international assistance. In parting advice to my successor, Amb. Tom Krajeski, I urged him to focus on the challenge of economic reform as his top priority. Fortunately, the Bush administration had created a vehicle by which such reform could be encouraged and supported. The Millennium Challenge identified exactly the kind of reforms required for Yemen to reverse its course and to win substantial support from the United States and the international community. "Qualify Yemen for the Millennium Challenge" was my succinct advice.

TURNING POINT: THE HOUTHI REBELLION

Even as I was departing, however, a serious, new challenge was already diverting Yemen's leadership from al Qaeda terrorism and reform. In June 2004 Sheikh Hussein Badraddin al-Houthi, the leader of an influential clan in the vicinity of Sa'dah near the Saudi border, organized protests and took up arms against the government. I had visited Sa'dah several times and knew it to be the cradle of Yemeni Shia Islam, which had dominated the politics of northern Yemen for centuries under the rule of Zaidi imams. My Yemeni driver Taha, himself a member of the imam's extended family, had pointed out the sites connected with the imam in Sa'dah and complained bitterly of ill treatment of the extended family after the imam's followers were defeated in 1960s by the forces of the new Yemeni republic. The Houthis were Hashemites tracing their ancestry to the Prophet Mohamed, and many believed that President Saleh, also a Zaidi but of modest origin, was unqualified to rule. I was also aware of growing Saudi influence in Sa'dah centered in the Dar al-Hadith Institute in nearby Dammaj, which fostered Wahhabism, a Saudi fundamentalist alternative to traditional Shia doctrine.[2]

Sheikh Hussein Badraddin al-Houthi organized both his protests and resistance through the Organization for Youthful Believers. They shocked the government by staging demonstrations in Sanaa in January 2003. At the center of their protest was criticism of the government for neglecting the Sa'dah region, but ideologically they favored a revival of Hashemite rule and criticized the inroads of Wahhabi influence and the Yemeni government's cooperation with the United States.[3] Media accounts often simplified the dispute as one between Shia and Sunni, as was occurring in Iraq, but neglected to note that President Saleh and much of his ruling establishment were themselves Shia. For its part, the government alleged an Iranian hand behind the rebellion but never provided evidence of significant support.

The government's response was largely military and its use of force often indiscriminate. What began as a revival of a Zaidi group and protest against government neglect gradually transformed into a widespread insurgency, which at times has touched the outskirts of Sanaa.[4] Five rounds of fighting have ensued. Qatar has attempted to mediate. Unlike in the civil war of the 1960s, Saudi Arabia has sided with the republic and entered the conflict directly when it felt its border and interests threatened. The fighting has caused widespread humanitarian suffering.[5] In late 2009 another one of many cease-fires was reached, and President Saleh declared the war over, but experts were skeptical that the peace would hold.[6]

TURNING POINT: THE SOUTHERN MOVEMENT

The discontent in Yemen's North eventually became mirrored in the South. Unification of North and South Yemen in 1990 had been one of President Saleh's historic achievements, and he had successfully defended it by force of arms in 1994. He had made an effort to reach out to southerners, generally better educated than their northern counterparts, by including them in the government but not his inner circle. Also, both Yemen's government and international development experts recognized Aden and Al Mukalla as engines for Yemeni economic development. During my tenure, competent governors were striving to develop those relatively prosperous areas, and the World Bank was focusing its development strategy on the major port cities because of their economic potential.[7] President Saleh visited the South frequently and usually spent the winter in residence in Aden. The Yemeni Socialist Party continued to function with relative freedom and gave political voice to southerners with a leftist bent.

Southern resentment of dominance by the North smoldered nevertheless. National identity can be a delicate shoot. The concentration of political power in the

North and in the hands of the president, his clan, and his tribe gradually became more and more resented.[8] Southerners particularly resented land grabs by the northern elite.[9] In May 2007 resentment began to take the form of a mass movement. Former military officers organized protests to highlight the insufficiency of pensions. The protests evolved into more general complaints about central government corruption and particularly the opaque control of Yemeni oil and gas resources that straddle the former border between North and South Yemen. Essentially nonviolent, the Southern Movement made a point of separating itself from al Qaeda and its affiliate the Islamic Army of Aden, which was located in the South and had long pursued a low-grade violent opposition to central authority. Ongoing protests were suppressed forcibly, engendering new grievances. Hisham Bashrahil, the editor in chief of Aden's respected newspaper *Al Ayyam,* was imprisoned. The defection of Tareq al-Fadhli, the scion of a prominent southern tribe, from President Saleh's camp in early 2010 added political momentum to the movement.[10] Al-Fadhli's change of allegiance appeared all the more significant because he had used his mujahideen connections to rally support for President Saleh against the South in suppressing the rebellion of 1994.

The Houthi rebellion in the North and the Southern Movement had strikingly difference origins and methods, but they were very similar in their critiques of the ruling power. Too much power had rested for too long in the hands of too few. The country's oil and gas wealth was being exhausted, with little accountability or public benefit. Resources flowed to the capital while the rest of the country felt neglected.

TURNING POINT: THE 2006 PRESIDENTIAL ELECTION

In the North and in the South, the central government reacted to what it perceived as essentially security challenges. However, the fundamental causes of these movements cried out for political and economic reforms. By Middle Eastern standards, Yemen's political system had a well-developed basis for such reform. Political parties were well established and active. Election mechanics were relatively sophisticated, and the Yemeni voters were enthusiastic. In the wake of the 2003 parliamentary election, Freedom House had improved Yemen's ranking to "partially free." The momentum for political evolution carried forward through the presidential election of 2006. President Saleh, unlike most of his Arab peers, ran against real opposition. Faisal bin Shamlan carried the banner for the Joint Meetings Parties, a new opposition grouping that included the Islamic party Islah, the Yemeni Socialist Party, and several minor parties. The campaign went well and included significant access to the media by the opposition. Saleh won handily with 77 percent of the vote, although polling during the campaign had raised the specter of defeat.[11] A relatively honest and competitive presidential election in the Middle East was a rare and noteworthy accomplishment.

Unfortunately, the tide of political reform then turned. That reform had always depended on the support of the president. Even a 23 percent opposition vote was apparently taken as a humiliation, and the uncertainty of a free and fair campaign may have been traumatic.[12] International encouragement had been coupled with a ruler's reluctance to produce political evolution. Since 2006 Yemen's leadership has appeared to rest on its laurels.

TURNING POINT: THE MILLENNIUM CHALLENGE SLIPS AWAY

On economic reform, little progress was made in the 2001–4 period. We recognized a linkage between security and development, and pioneered models of how government services could be extended to the remote tribal areas of Yemen. Under the rubric of MEPI, we also engaged Yemeni civil society on a piecemeal basis. The heavy lifting, however, was left to our successors. Of course, the primary challenge lay with the Yemeni government and particularly the economic ministries in Sanaa. The World Bank engaged ably with its staff in Sanaa and Washington, and the IMF sent teams periodically to review Yemen's progress. I was convinced, however, that the United States could play a catalytic role and that we had a suitable vehicle in the Millennium Challenge, which linked reform in seventeen political and economic areas to substantial U.S. development assistance.

My successor labored mightily. As was typical in Yemen, progress was made in fits and starts. In November 2005 Yemen was denied Millennium Challenge threshold status because of increasing corruption.[13] The announcement's timing was particularly unfortunate as it coincided with President Saleh's visit to Washington. To their credit, both Yemeni and American reformers persisted. Finally, on September 12, 2007, the Millennium Challenge Corporation approved a $20.6 million threshold program for Yemen. The sum was modest, but the principle of linking tangible assistance with specific reforms was of the first importance.

Sadly, it was not to be. Before the program could be launched, Jamal al-Badawi, one of the masterminds of the attack on the USS *Cole* who had again escaped from prison, surrendered to Yemeni authorities. In an affront to their U.S. counterterrorism partner, al-Badawi was released to house arrest two days later under lenient terms of the Yemenis' surrender program. He was later reimprisoned after American protests but never seriously punished for his role in the murder of seventeen U.S. Navy sailors.[14]

A bad situation was made worse by the U.S. reaction. Looking to demonstrate its displeasure, the U.S. administration cancelled the Millennium Challenge program. The linkage was understandable on an emotional level but betrayed shaky logic. In undermining Yemeni reform, the United States was acting against its own best interests. Economic reformers in Yemen, an endangered species, were to pay the price.[15]

The embassy's modest development program also suffered from neglect and a lack of focus. The funds from the sale of surplus American agricultural commodities gradually dried up, and disagreements on allocating the funds stalled the program. Traditional economic assistance funds were at token levels: $8 million in FY 2006, $12 million in FY 2007, and $9 million in FY 2008.[16] Lack of resources made it difficult to pursue development in al Qaeda's desired safe havens Ma'rib, Al Jawf, and Shabwah. The president's hospital in Ma'rib did begin operations with the young trainees recruited from Ma'rib and trained in Sanaa. However, an admirable effort by the embassy to negotiate professional management of the facility failed. The small clinic at Madghil continued to serve as a model of what might have been.[17] Sheikh Rabish pronounced himself fully satisfied with U.S. support and even proposed his own daughter as a participant in a new midwife program.[18]

The venerable Islah sheikh Abdullah al-Ahmar had said the tribes wanted "roads, hospitals, schools, and jobs." Instead, NDI undertook a dubious program of outreach to the tribes under the rubric of dispute settlement.[19] The president reacted negatively to this perceived meddling in tribal politics. The embassy found its movement in tribal areas increasingly restricted and also lacked the resources to back the government in making tangible improvements in the daily life of the tribes. Parts of Yemen that had been made safe for development were soon to become increasingly safe for al Qaeda instead.

TURNING POINT: THE AL QAEDA JAILBREAK

Yemeni counterterrorism efforts, supported by the United States, had slowly removed al Qaeda's key operatives from the battlefield by 2004. They were incarcerated in the PSO's "maximum security" prison in Sanaa. In February 2006 twenty-three al Qaeda prisoners escaped via a tunnel dug from the prison to a nearby mosque.[20] The prisoners, including al Qaeda operatives who had learned tunneling techniques in Afghanistan, had been allowed to group together in prison and to exercise a large measure of control over their section of the prison to the extent of excluding guards from it. The escapees had outside assistance in some of their tunneling equipment and probably in their flight after the break-out. Clearly PSO leadership had been negligent. President Saleh was deeply angered.[21] In July a dozen PSO officers were convicted of collusion by a military court.[22]

Among the escapees, the Americans naturally focused on *Cole* attacker Jamal al-Badawi and Jaber Elbaneh, an indicted Yemeni American long wanted by the FBI. Actually of more significance was the escape of the future leadership of al Qaeda in Yemen, Nasir al-Wahayshi, Qasim al-Raymi, Hizam Majali, and Muhammad al-'Umda.[23] For some months, the al Qaeda escapees lay low. They reorganized themselves and developed relative safe havens in Yemen's remote tribal areas. They developed a strategy that initially focused on two of Yemen's economic supports—oil/gas and tourism.

In September 2007 al Qaeda in Yemen launched its initial attacks against oil and gas facilities in Ma'rib and the Hadramawt, the vast province northeast of Shabwah. The dual suicide attacks failed. The following spring, al Qaeda succeeded in assassinating Ali Mahmud Qasaylah, the chief criminal investigator in Ma'rib. By early July the target was tourism. There was a suicide attack on a convoy of Spanish tourists in Ma'rib in which ten persons died, followed six months later by an attack on Belgian tourists in the Hadramawt in which four persons died.[24]

In early 2008, al Qaeda in Yemen found its voice with the initiation of an electronic journal, *Sada al-Malahim* (*Echo of Battle*). This initiative indicated a sophisticated attention to defining and promoting its ideology and foreshadowed increasingly effective use of media and the Internet. By March al Qaeda in Yemen undertook its first attack on U.S. targets. The American embassy was attacked by mortars that caused no American casualties and little damage but injured dozens in the neighboring girls' school.[25] In the 2001–4 period, al Qaeda had envisioned a similar attack but never pulled it off. A month later, al Qaeda fired three mortars at the Al Hadda residential compound in Sanaa where U.S. embassy employees and other Westerners resided. This event triggered the ordered departure of nonessential U.S. embassy staff and family members. Six months later, on September 17, 2008, al Qaeda attackers using two vehicle bombs and suicide vests attacked the embassy's entrance, killing eighteen persons, including one American.[26] The scale of this attack, which rivaled that of the attack on the *Cole*, was a wake-up call for all of Washington.

During this period, Yemeni authorities had conducted a successful raid against an al Qaeda cell in the Hadramawt, killing five al Qaeda operatives and seizing a number of weapons, including mortars, explosives, and material for building car bombs.[27] On balance, however, the State Department judged that "the [Yemeni] government's response to the terrorist threat was intermittent and its ability to pursue and prosecute terrorists remained weak due to a number of shortcomings."[28]

This new version of al Qaeda in Yemen, however, had larger ambitions. In January 2009 it announced a merger with the remnants of the al Qaeda group in Saudi Arabia and thus formed Al Qaeda in the Arabian Peninsula (AQAP). In quick succession, an AQAP suicide bomber killed four South Korean tourists and their Yemeni guide in the Hadramawt on March 18 and then quickly mounted another suicide attack three days later against the South Korean officials investigating the first attack. These attacks were still within Yemen. By August, however, an AQAP suicide bomber traveled to Saudi Arabia and gained access to the head of Saudi's counterterrorism effort, Mohamed bin Nayyif, who narrowly escaped assassination.[29] Within two months, Saudi security forces also intercepted a car containing three other AQAP operatives and killed two of them.

By this time, U.S. officials had significantly ramped up counterterrorism assistance to Yemen. The Obama administration correctly identified Yemen as a counterterrorism priority from its outset.[30] As in the early 2000s, a procession of high-level U.S. visitors came to Sanaa, including Gen. David Petraeus,[31] NSC counterterrorism adviser John Brennan, State counterterrorism coordinator Daniel Benjamin, and Assistant Secretary of State Jeff Feltman.[32]

General Petraeus's visit of July 26, 2009, was particularly notable. In its wake, President Saleh dispatched his nephew ʿAmmar Muhammad, the principal deputy in the National Security Bureau,[33] to Maʾrib to counter growing al Qaeda influence there. In an episode reminiscent of the failed attempt to capture Abu Assem al-Mekki in December 2001, the government forces mistakenly shelled a tribal house rather than an al Qaeda safe house. The resulting firefight cost the military several tanks and a number of killed and wounded. Seven Yemeni soldiers ended up as al Qaeda prisoners. Government efforts with the media to minimize the setback were disputed by al Qaeda, which produced a video portraying its success in the "Battle of Maʾrib" and showing the captured soldiers to buttress its claims.[34]

Yemeni counterterrorism efforts proved somewhat more successful by the end of the year. On December 17, Yemeni forces in Sanaa arrested fourteen individuals accused of supporting al Qaeda and also killed three al Qaeda operatives in the Arhab tribal area northeast of the capital.[35] On the same day, air attacks were conducted against a reported al Qaeda training facility in Abyan. The raid killed a number of al Qaeda suspects as well as a number of civilian women and children. Deputy Prime Minister for Defense and Security Affairs Rashad al-Alimi reported to Parliament on December 23 that an investigation was being conducted into the deaths of the civilians.[36]

On December 22 and 24, air strikes were carried out against targets in Shabwah resulting in the death of a handful of al Qaeda suspects.[37] The target was believed to be an al Qaeda training camp, but again a significant number of civilian women and children were among the casualties. While the United States welcomed these actions in principle, its spokesmen declined to comment in detail on any support provided.

In two regards, these air strikes were significantly less effective than the strike that eliminated Abu Ali al-Harithi in November 2002. First, they failed to eliminate any significant al Qaeda leaders. Second, they reportedly entailed significant civilian casualties, which risked rallying support for al Qaeda among the tribes in the targeted areas. Contrast, for example, the tribal claims arising from the December 2009 strikes with the lack of such claims in the aftermath of the Abu Ali strike in 2002. In at least one instance, the strikes reportedly relied on cruise missiles,[38] a far less discriminating instrument than well-trained Yemeni special forces or even a Predator missile.

In AQAP, Yemen and the United States confront a significantly more potent and more ambitious enemy than the organization that was virtually destroyed between 2001 and 2004. The al Qaeda virus in Yemen has mutated in several dangerous ways. First, the Christmas Day plot demonstrated AQAP's global ambitions and global reach. In its statements, AQAP has set for itself the ambitious agenda of penetrating U.S. defenses and striking U.S. interests worldwide. In past such statements, AQAP has made good on its words. Second, through its electronic journal, AQAP effectively articulated its developing ideology and enhanced its ability to radicalize and attract discontented individuals, including non-Arabs such as Umar Farouk Abdulmuttalib, the Nigerian who undertook the attack on Northwest Airlines flight 253. Third, in its media depiction of the Battle of Ma'rib, AQAP has successfully challenged the Yemeni government's quasimonopoly on information and enhanced its credibility at the expense of the government. Fourth, AQAP apparently has made inroads into some tribal groups, a key objective. Tribal cooperation was not forthcoming during the Battle of Ma'rib. Air strikes on al Qaeda objectives have triggered condemnations by the tribes affected. There are few, if any, reports of tribal assistance to government counterterrorism operations.

This new, more potent strain of al Qaeda requires a much more ambitious response than that which successfully countered al Qaeda in Yemen between 2001 and 2004. Policymakers in Washington, who were already concerned with Yemen prior to Christmas 2009, significantly escalated their attention thereafter. Assistant Secretary of State Feltman laid out for the House Committee on Foreign Affairs on February 3, 2010, "a new, more holistic Yemen policy that not only seeks to address security and counterterrorism concerns, but also the profound political, economic and social challenges that help Al-Qaeda and related affiliates to operate and flourish." In this regard, Assistant Secretary Feltman noted dramatic increases in development and security assistance: from $17 million in FY '08 and $40 million in FY '09 to $67 million in FY '10 and $106 million in FY '11.[39] The Obama strategy has much to recommend: it recognizes the connection between security and development, particularly in the deprived areas of Yemen where al Qaeda aims to create a safe haven; it presses from political and economic reform on the part of the Yemeni government; and it seeks to enlist support from the international community and particularly Yemen's neighbors in the Gulf Cooperation Council (GCC) in helping Yemen address the overwhelming problems it faces. The challenges—and they are formidable—will be in implementation.

CHALLENGE 1: CAPTURE OR KILL AL QAEDA TERRORISTS

The initial security response to AQAP in Yemen has not proven particularly effective and has entailed potentially serious political risks. Despite Yemeni security operations, notably in December 2009, AQAP's leadership remains intact. While some lesser operatives have been either killed or captured, Nasir al-Wahayshi and his deputy, Sa'id al-Shihri, remain at large. There is a parallel here with al Qaeda Central operating from the tribal areas of Pakistan and Osama bin Laden and Ayman al-Zawahiri. Moreover, recent attempts to eliminate AQAP's leadership with air strikes and/or cruise missiles have reportedly caused significant civilian casualties. From 2001 to 2004, operations by Yemeni forces, particularly CSF, proved to be the most effective tool for capturing or killing al Qaeda terrorists who refused to surrender. An alternative, which proved both effective and highly discriminating as used in Yemen, was the Predator drone. In either case, success depends not only on a well-trained and well-equipped counterterrorism force or an appropriate technology, but also on actionable and accurate intelligence.

If captured, al Qaeda terrorists must face more certain justice than in the past. The 2003 al Qaeda jailbreak in Aden revealed a fundamental flaw in Yemen's security system. The jailbreak from Sanaa in 2006 was proof that this flaw had not been corrected. The State Department has previously stressed a need to strengthen Yemen's counterterrorism law. Surely a broader approach is called for that includes effective incarceration.

CHALLENGE 2: DENY AL QAEDA TRIBAL PROTECTION

When Abu Ali al-Harithi was killed in 2002, his kin made no claim on the Yemeni government. The Harithis in effect repudiated his al Qaeda connection. In contrast, media reports suggest that Anwar Aulaqi, currently sought in connection with the November 2009 Fort Hood shootings and the Christmas Day 2009 plot, enjoys the protection of his tribe in Shabwah. More broadly al Qaeda appears to be engaged in a strategy of not only financial inducement but also intermarriage into Yemeni tribes in order to re-create the success it has had in Afghanistan and Pakistan.

From 2001 to 2004, we found that Yemeni tribes had relatively simple priorities: health, jobs, roads, and schools. Often the need could be addressed with modest resources, and, if done properly, the local community would support the project materially. The more significant challenge was obtaining buy-in from the relevant government ministries so recurrent costs—staff, supplies, and maintenance—would be covered. In contrast, NDI's subsequent program aimed at dispute resolution among the tribes appears a misguided attempt by outsiders that was misunderstood by the tribes and deemed a threat by the central government. As the United States vastly expands its USAID efforts in Yemen, history suggests that it should take care to respond tangibly to legitimate needs as perceived by the tribes and in a way so as to enhance the role and responsibility of the central government.[40]

The 2001–4 experience also suggests that remote control from Sanaa is not the best way to understand and address the problems of the tribes in Yemen's deprived areas. In his first meeting on counterterrorism, Secretary Powell warned against the United States adopting a bunker mentality in responding to the al Qaeda threat. Risks, particularly those associated with travel, should be managed, but they cannot be eliminated. Embassy Sanaa should be staffed robustly and not primarily with intelligence and military personnel, but with State and other experts able to address the broader problems of Yemen.

CHALLENGE 3: RESTORE MOMENTUM FOR REFORM

Yemeni reform will not happen without Yemenis themselves taking initiatives *and* the international community providing inducements and support. Yemen's political evolution from the late '90s up to 2006 showed that Yemenis valued democracy and excelled at reform of their electoral process. Yemen has been a leader in the Arab world in this regard and should adopt further reform as a special vocation. The United States has tools that have proven effective in the past, such as NDI and MEPI. From 2003 to 2006, high-level U.S. attention, like President Saleh's invitation to the G-8 Summit, proved effective in building a will to reform at the highest levels of the Yemeni government.

Yemen's failure to qualify for the Millennium Challenge remains a significant piece of unfinished business related to economic reform. In its FY '09 scorecard, the Millennium Challenge Corporation surprisingly shows Yemen above average in "Control of Corruption," which reflected establishment of a corruption board and reform of tendering law in Yemen. In many other areas—regulatory quality, business start-up, fiscal policy, rule of law, political rights, rule of law, immunization rates—Yemen is on the verge of exceeding the median score. Economic reform is far from hopeless. What is needed is a partnership between Yemeni reformers from within, and U.S. and international inducement and support from without.

CHALLENGE 4: CREATE A REGIONAL FRAMEWORK
TO RESPOND TO A REGIONAL THREAT

Al Qaeda in the Arabian Peninsula has boldly stated its framework and objectives in a way that transcends Yemen. Those who would effectively frustrate those objectives need to take a page from AQAP's playbook. Yemen's economic problems cannot be addressed without redefining their context. In ensuring security for Europe, the EU has consistently made strategic choices to include in its project peripheral states with economic, security, and political problems. In the aftermath of Franco, Spain and Portugal were addressed. After the fall of the Soviet Union, Eastern European states found a home. The states of the Arabian Peninsula similarly need a strategic vision for Yemen.

The Gulf Cooperation Council (GCC) per se is unlikely to provide that framework. It is a club for rich monarchies, and Yemen is neither rich nor a monarchy. Yet, the GCC has shown a willingness to accord Yemen special status in selected committees, and the evolution of this special status holds promise. In a significant way, populous Yemen and the labor-seeking Gulf states complement each other. Yemenis currently do well in Gulf police forces and in small enterprises. As Henry Ford found on his assembly lines, Yemenis are excellent workers when given opportunity. In theory, Yemen also offers Gulf states an attractive market and investment opportunities if those investments are sufficiently encouraged and protected. Yemen's climate, landscapes, history, and culture may well give this generation, and perhaps more so future generations of Arab travelers, relief from oppressive Gulf weather and provide windows on the past glory of Islam. In integrating Yemen with its neighbors, no country has a greater interest or greater leverage than Saudi Arabia. A Saudi vision of a more secure and prosperous peninsula is to be encouraged and supported practically. AQAP has thrown down a gauntlet. Not only Yemen, but also the Arabian Peninsula as a whole, needs to reflect and respond.

CONCLUSION

The al Qaeda virus in Yemen is long-standing and at times virulent. If not addressed, it will spread not only throughout the Arabian Peninsula, but also globally as it finds vulnerabilities in international defenses. Yemeni "antibodies" are far and away the most effective, least costly, and most sustainable response to this threat. U.S. "boots on the ground," except in support of Yemeni efforts, will be counterproductive. Al Qaeda would welcome foreign intervention that will support its narrative of "occupation" and cause Yemen's tribes, religious establishment, and ultimately its people to accord al Qaeda the status of "resistance." As the United States assists the Yemeni government in responding to this infection, it has the delicate tasks of strengthening the role of the central government and encouraging essential services so as to win support from Yemen's tribes, especially in remote areas, and address the underlying conditions—corruption and lack of opportunity—that alienate Yemen's population from its government. Al Qaeda has learned the lessons of the past and adapted successfully. Yemen's government and the United States are challenged to understand what has gone before and adapt as well.

NOTES

INTRODUCTION

1. Similarly, U.S. administrations during the Cold War addressed the threat of communism and obscured important schisms and rivalries.

2. See, for example, Richard A. Clarke, *Against All Enemies: Inside America's War on Terror* (New York: Free Press, 2004).

3. Unrelated groups may indeed constitute separate threats to U.S. interests, but each threat should be addressed on its own merits by appropriate means.

4. David Kilcullen also makes use of this device in his insightful book *The Accidental Guerrilla: Fighting Small Wars in the Midst of a Big One* (New York: Oxford University Press, 2009), 34–38.

5. The literature on this subject is vast, and I do not pretend to have absorbed it all. However, from thirty-three years of working in the Middle East and two subsequent years of study and teaching at Princeton University, I have found foreign occupations to be particularly problematic—in Lebanon spawning Hezbollah, in Palestine spawning Hamas, in Kashmir spawning Lashkar-e-Tayyiba, in the mandate of Palestine spawning the Irgun and the Stern Gang, and in Iraq spawning al Qaeda (post-2003 invasion). For a strong empirical argument along these lines, see Robert Pape, *Dying to Win: The Strategic Logic of Suicide Terrorism* (New York: Random House, 2005).

6. Essentially, I believe al Qaeda's ideology is a response to a perception that the Islamic world is under attack and occupied by an array of enemies. It was graphically depicted on a mujahideen map that I found in Islamabad's Friday market

(*suq al jum'a*) in the late 1990s. The Islamic world was assaulted on many fronts: America's military presence in the Gulf, India's presence in Kashmir, Israel's occupation of Arab territories, Russia's repression of Chechnya, and China's dominance of the Uigurs in western China. Following the successful jihad to expel the Soviets from Afghanistan, al Qaeda's mission was to inspire Muslims to oppose foreign occupations or domination throughout the Islamic world and provide a "base" for this armed struggle. Corrupt and complicit regimes became primary targets of the jihad.

7. Al Qaeda might well argue that one man's virus is another man's antibody, however. How the population views the matter (e.g., who are the foreigners?) proves critical, as will be addressed in the account that follows.

8. While safe havens are the focus of this account, it is important to acknowledge the importance of counterterrorism efforts along two other lines of effort: first, disrupting and defeating the al Qaeda network beyond its safe havens (or its global operating, financing, recruiting, and logistical network), and second, addressing the al Qaeda ideology through effective strategic communications such as President Obama's Cairo address to the Islamic world, rejection of torture, and closing down of Guantánamo Bay. In terms of our graphic, think of one line of effort directed at the al Qaeda viruses as they spread globally and another line addressing its radicalizing ideology. Both supplement related efforts against al Qaeda safe havens.

9. Theorists of jihad even identify a category of operations—vexation operations—designed to goad the United States into direct military actions to destabilize an area and eventually entice American forces into prolonged conflicts that will bleed the United States physically and financially. See Abu Bakr Naji, "The Management of Savagery: The Most Critical Stage through Which the Umma Will Pass," translated by William McCants for the John M. Olin Institute for Strategic Studies at Harvard University, May 23, 2006, 24, 25, 45, 46.

10. Unless otherwise noted, all economic/social statistics are from the World Bank.

11. Oil and gas represent one third of gross domestic product, three quarters of government revenues, and 90 percent of exports. But reserves are rapidly being depleted, and even with the new addition of liquefied natural gas, prospects are poor.

12. Mohammed al-Maitami, "Economic Challenges to Stability," in *The Battle for Yemen: Al Qaeda and the Struggle for Stability*, ed. Ramzy Mardini (Washington: Jamestown Foundation, 2010), 211. Al-Maitami also reports that the World Bank

estimates that the average Yemeni household spends 11 percent of its household budget on khat.

13. See, for example, the *New York Times* editorial "Now Yemen," December 30, 2009.

14. In 2003 Transparency International first surveyed Perceptions of Corruption in Yemen. With a score of 2.6, Yemen then ranked 88 out of 133 countries. In 2009 the score had declined to 2.1, and Yemen ranked 154 out of 180 countries. Because of a large standard deviation, the decline is indicative, not definitive.

15. The Western media tend to see the Houthi rebellion through the Iraq lens with emphasis on Sunni versus Shia. However, the leaders of both are Zaidi and therefore Shia. More will be said of this in the afterword.

16. See Human Rights Watch, *No Direction Home: Returns from Guantanamo to Yemen*, March 28, 2009.

17. I am indebted to Michael W. S. Ryan, senior research associate at the Jamestown Foundation, for pointing out Naji's thinking on Yemen as a safe haven at the Jamestown Foundation's program on Yemen on April 15, 2010. See Abu Bakr Naji, "The Management of Savagery," 37–39.

18. Ibid., 38.

CHAPTER 1. AL QAEDA STRIKES A BLOW

1. Of the briefing, Secretary Powell commented, "A major component of the briefing was al Qaida's growing threat to U.S. interests and Afghanistan as a safe haven. As a matter of fact, that part of the briefing got my attention. So much so, that later I asked Mr. Armitage to get directly involved as soon as he was sworn in. And he did." Statement to the 9/11 Commission, March 23, 2004.

2. The Department of State ceased publishing statistics in 2005 after a mistake in 2004 led to charges that the administration was manipulating them in order to boost President Bush's reelection. However, the statistics were always compiled by CIA analysts and were not subject to State or other manipulation.

3. *Black Hawk Down* is Mark Bowden's account of the operation to capture Somali warlord Mohamed Farrah Aidid on October 3 and 4, 1993. The operation miscarried and resulted in the deaths of eighteen U.S. military personnel, losses that prompted the Clinton administration's decision to leave Somalia. See Bowden, *Black Hawk Down: A Story of Modern War* (New York: Atlantic Monthly, 1999).

4. A contrary argument is that an unwelcome U.S. military presence in an Islamic country is viewed as a form of foreign occupation that is the primary spur to suicide terrorism. See Pape, *Dying to Win*.

5. National Commission on Terrorist Attacks upon the United States, *The 9/11 Commission Report: Final Report of the National Commission on Terrorist Attacks upon the United States* (New York: W. W. Norton, 2004), 314.

6. At that time, I was NSC's director for the Middle East and saw how that attack became a defining moment for the Clinton administration.

7. The Arabic sentiment tracked one of my father's favorite expressions as he moved us from fence painting to post-hole digging: "A change of jobs is like a vacation."

CHAPTER 2. PARTNER OR TARGET?

1. See Jeffrey Gettleman, "Yemen, Once a Magnet, Now Expels Terrorists," *Los Angeles Times*, October 10, 2001.

2. Foreign Service Officer Georgia J. Debell handled the extraordinarily complicated negotiations, which included gaining consensus from disparate owners seeking to leverage their parcels into financial windfalls. Administrative officers, such as Debell, receive little credit, but their tenacity is essential in creating safe environments for the diplomacy, security, intelligence, and law enforcement work that follows.

3. In the aftermath of the East Africa embassy bombings in 1998, FBI investigators flooded Nairobi and Dar es Salaam and quickly cracked the case. Based on that success, FBI investigators led by O'Neill tried a similar approach to the bombing of the *Cole* in 2000 but ran into Yemeni restrictions. As in all Arab countries, Yemeni officials and the public highly value sovereignty. In this case, that motivation was reinforced by official concern of links between al Qaeda terrorists and government officials.

4. "All United States Government personnel (other than those elements and personnel in country under the command of a U.S. area commander or on the staff of an international organization) must obtain country clearance before entering the Republic of Yemen on official business. You may refuse country clearance or may place conditions or restrictions on visiting personnel as you determine necessary." President Bush's letter of instruction to author, August 6, 2001.

5. One of the more scurrilous opposition newspapers mistook Sandy for the ambassador's wife and published an article condemning "Mrs. Ambassador's" language classes as the "brainwashing" of Yemeni women.

6. The noms de guerre of Qaed Salim Sinan and Mohamed Hamdi al-Ahdal, respectively.

7. Al Qaeda operatives often included in their nicknames references to their origins: al-Masri (of Egypt), al-Libby (of Libya), and so forth. The usage is practical; seemingly half of Arab males are named Mohamed, and hence Mohamed the Tunisian is a useful distinction. Also, in reiterating origins, al Qaeda stressed its international character.

8. Suddam and Sanibani heard the most sensitive discussions throughout the next three years with never a leak. One had to admire their discretion while regretting a media so controlled by authority.

9. In the event, Melara opted to stay; served a full tour, including service on the chem-bio response team; and earned a Meritorious Honor Award for her service.

10. Chance, and his eventual successor, Tim Laas, were extraordinarily dedicated to protecting the embassy and its community, and spent many nights on office cots on the job. Occasionally, they needed to be ordered to go home and rest. To them goes much of the credit that no official Americans suffered harm from terrorism in my three years in Yemen.

11. President Saleh certainly didn't mind our security measures. On a subsequent occasion, he and I reviewed an aerial photo of the embassy compound, and the president veered the conversation to where he would place sharpshooters on its walls to enhance its defenses.

12. Jambiyyas are the curved daggers worn by all Yemeni males in traditional garb. Young Yemenis adopt one as a mark of manhood. As a fashion item, they are roughly equivalent to a tie in Western dress.

13. To my knowledge, Sheikh al-Ahmar had never visited that locale, at least not since 1967 when Israel occupied East Jerusalem. I knew it well, on the other hand, from my tour as a vice consul in Jerusalem.

14. For a sympathetic view of khat, see Tim Mackintosh-Smith, *Yemen: Travels in Dictionary Land* (London: John Murray, 1997), 16–28.

15. Indeed, I risked offending many hosts in following this principle during three years in Yemen. Initially, I publicized the position, but Brad Hanson came to me one day to report that the ambassador's moralizing on the subject was being resented as superior. I thereafter became tacit, but no less a teetotaler.

16. Henry Ford Sr. was particularly impressed with Yemeni workers on his car assembly lines and wrote to the British consul general in Aden to recruit fifty or more additional Yemeni workers, according to Abdulhakim Alsadah, Yemen's honorary consul in Michigan. Former Ford CEO Jacques Nasser told him the company retains a copy of Ford's letter.

17. *Mafraj* means vantage point and refers to the large penthouse area in a traditional Yemeni house, where khat is chewed and guests are entertained.

18. Patrick E. Tyler, "In Washington, a Struggle to Define the Next Fight," *New York Times,* December 2, 2001.

19. Gettleman, "Yemen Once a Magnet."

20. Khalilzad was ubsequently appointed ambassador to Afghanistan, Iraq, and the UN.

21. Subsequently appointed ambassador to Pakistan and Iraq.

22. Most helpful was Paul Dresch, *Tribes, Government, and History in Yemen* (New York: Oxford University Press, 1989).

23. The upper (appointed) legislative body, the Shura Council, was headed by Abdul Aziz Abdul Ghani, another USAID scholarship beneficiary.

24. ATA funded counterterrorism training for foreign security forces. TIP funded computers and databases so countries could spot terrorists transiting through airports, seaports, or land crossings. Both were administered by S/CT, where Yemen had strong support.

CHAPTER 3. A MEETING OF MINDS

1. There were exceptions. Dick had particularly close relations with Israel, which caused him to run afoul of arms transfer regulations as director of political military affairs in State. His faltering career was saved by Brent Scowcroft, who took him into the NSC as senior director for global issues—one of which was counterterrorism. Dick also had extremely close personal relations with the ruling family of Abu Dhabi, which he used to good effect.

CHAPTER 4. GROWING PAINS

1. Feisal Abu Ras, a Yemeni parliamentarian from Al Jawf, recounted to me his boyhood spent largely in Egypt as a hostage; the Egyptians had taken him from the powerful Abu Ras tribe during their attempt to control Yemen in the 1960s. Far from being emotionally scarred or embittered, Feisal chalked up the experience as part of an elite Yemeni's "education."

2. The Islamic Army of Aden was a homegrown terrorist group with loose ideological links to al Qaeda (see *Patterns of Global Terrorism 2002*). Additionally, Abu Hamza al-Masri later became the subject of a U.S. extradition request in 2004. The British eventually charged Al-Masri on October 19, 2004, for sixteen offenses including encouraging murder, stirring up race hatred, and possessing a

terrorist document. He was convicted on eleven charges on February 7, 2006 and sentenced to seven years in prison following which he faces extradition to the United States (see Stewart Tendler, "Abu Hamza Accused of Inciting Hate and murder," *The Sunday Times*, October 20, 2004, http://www.timesonline.co.uk/ article/0,,2-1319188,00.html; and Wikipedia entry "Abu Hamza al-Masri."

3. *Terror in Yemen: Where To?* (Sanaa: 26th September Publications, 2002), 16.

4. This policy is often misunderstood as precluding negotiations with terrorists. In fact, engaging kidnappers in a negotiation is often a "best practice" to argue for surrender of the kidnappers or at least release of the victims. Substantive concessions, not negotiations themselves, are forbidden.

5. The kidnappers had no connection to al Qaeda and did not even represent their tribe. Rather, they were young hotheads freelancing.

6. Yemen has three main political parties: the ruling General People's Congress, the Islamic opposition party Islah, and the Yemeni Socialist Party, which originated in South Yemen's Marxist tradition.

7. "Yemen Confronting Terrorism: Selections from Speeches and Statements of President Ali Abdullah Saleh," Office of the President, March 2003, 85–86.

8. The house's telephone number linked Khallad bin Attash, who had been instrumental in the *Cole* attack, to the Kuala Lumpur meeting that involved the 9/11 conspirators. See George Tenet, *At the Center of the Storm: My Years at the CIA* (New York: HarperCollins, 2007), 197. *The 9/11 Commission Report* also identifies "Khallad" as Tawfiq bin Attash and as Waleed bin Attash, 434.

9. *Terror in Yemen*, 18–19. Tribal sources subsequently denied to an American journalist and researcher that a sonic boom triggered the clash without clarifying what did.

10. The operation was also reported in the *New York Times* on December 20, 2001: "A Nation Challenged: Pursuing Al Qaeda; Yemen Adds Troops in Battle to Capture Suspects."

11. Operation Enduring Freedom was originally Secretary of Defense Rumsfeld's designation of the Afghan campaign. See Bob Woodward, *Bush at War* (New York: Simon & Schuster), 135. It was later applied to the war on terror far beyond Afghanistan.

12. President Saleh took particular satisfaction in receiving VIPs in the former residence of the British High Commissioner in Aden.

13. The U.S. Air Force later assessed the airworthiness of Yemen's helicopter fleet, including the presidential helicopter. All failed miserably.

14. This rapport did not blind the agents to Yemeni shortcomings. Lead agent Ali H. Soufan has been candid in his assessment of Yemeni cooperation. See Soufan, "Coddling Terrorists in Yemen," *Washington Post*, May 17, 2008.

15. On the embassy country team, legal attachés represent the Department of Justice, including the FBI. They coordinate law enforcement activities with the host country.

16. Al-Nashiri was captured in the United Arab Emirates in November 2002 and handed over to the United States. His interrogation confirmed the extensive FBI case against him for the attack on the *Cole* (see *Patterns of Global Terrorism 2002*, 62).

17. Details of al Qaeda plotting in Yemen during this period became public during the trial of the surviving members of the al Qaeda cell in 2004.

18. In 2005 Yemen's oil exports were worth about $3.1 billion or roughly 70 percent of government revenue. See Department of State, "Background Note: Yemen," November 19, 2010, http://www.state.gov/r/pa/ei/bgn/35836.htm.

19. Fawaz al-Rabi'a later achieved notoriety by being placed by the FBI on its Most Wanted Terrorists list. He was a key operative in not only the spring 2002 bombings in Sanaa, but also an attack on the Hunt Oil Company's helicopter that November and a plot to assassinate me.

20. Statement by the Sympathizers with Al Qaeda, April 10, 2002.

21. PISCES (Personal Identification Secure Comparison and Evaluation System) is software for creating and managing watch lists.

22. Admiral Loy subsequently served as Deputy Secretary of Homeland Security from 2003 to 2005.

23. Willis, who specialized in training, was later tapped to train the Transportation Safety Administration forces in American airports and left Yemen for that job.

24. S/CT's Mark Thompson and James Webb also made notable contributions.

25. Both CENTCOM and other U.S. agencies were engaged.

26. "Remarks by the President on the Six-Month Anniversary of the September 11th Attacks," Office of the Press Secretary, March 11, 2002.

27. American special forces personnel are meant to have foreign language capabilities to operate and train in foreign environments. In fact, except for the rare Arab American recruit, our trainers had very limited ability to communicate except in English, which left them reliant on the Jordanians, who spoke English well, or Yemenis, who spoke English poorly if at all. Naturally, misunderstandings and suspicions multiplied.

CHAPTER 5. NO SECURITY WITHOUT DEVELOPMENT

1. The 9/11 Commission adopted an estimate of ten thousand to twenty thousand fighters trained by al Qaeda in Afghan camps between 1996 and 2001. See *The 9/11 Commission Report*, 67.

2. Saleh's reference was primarily to Ma'rib. Based on patterns of terrorist activity, we expanded our concern to two contiguous governorates: Shabwah, where Abu Ali was based, and the vast remote province of Al Jawf, which bordered Saudi Arabia and where Abu Assem operated. Khawlan, which lay between Sanaa and Ma'rib, was renowned for kidnapping and also received special attention as did 'Amran and later Abyan in the south, where the Islamic Army of Aden was centered.

3. Unfortunately, Yemen's developmentally correct policy statements usually represented a veneer that overlay profoundly ineffectual and corrupt practices. In turn, most international donors talked development aid but contributed relatively few resources. This "theater" allowed officials from both sides to appear significantly engaged in development. The ordinary Yemeni saw few results, and both Yemeni and donor credibility suffered.

4. Al-Arhabi became deputy prime minister and minister of planning and international cooperation in 2006.

5. At one point, our embassy attempted to hire a bright, young Yemeni woman from the Social Fund's ranks but could not match her compensation.

6. In 2004 the Social Fund hosted an international delegation from developing countries that came to study its successful practices.

7. Mac worked as a WAE. This program allows the State Department to tap the expertise of retired officers and allowed us to jumpstart not only development work in Sanaa, but also public diplomacy and to maintain consular services. See chapter 8.

8. *Qamari* means "moon-shaped" in Arabic.

9. Like much of what we did, the branding of U.S. projects proved controversial. The Yemeni government preferred that the Yemeni people credit it, not foreigners. Many donors also eschewed credit for their good works. Such an approach produced interesting results. I once asked the Saudi ambassador why Yemeni public opinion favored Iraq, not Saudi Arabia or Kuwait in the first Gulf War. An important part of the problem, he opined, was that his government had undertaken its significant aid program quietly and the average Yemeni had little knowledge of how much good work the Saudis had done in Yemen.

10. During my seven years in Egypt, I had been struck by the Aswan Dam phenomenon by which the developmentally correct U.S. assistance program generally received less credit from the Egyptian population than grandiose but dubious projects such as the Soviet's dam across the Nile River at Aswan or even the Japanese-built Cairo Opera House (the seats of which were designed to accommodate Asian, not Middle Eastern, posteriors).

11. A previous German ambassador was the exception. She reputedly relied on traditional tribal respect for women to travel freely in remote areas, to the consternation of Yemeni security officials.

12. Like a Greek chorus, the Yemeni opposition and independent media routinely bemoaned my travels to Ma'rib as interference in Yemeni internal affairs. The embassy rejoined that our effort was based on the president's request and fully coordinated with the government. We also invited along media representatives to witness and report our activities.

13. Wags dubbed these plastic bags floating in the breeze "the national bird of Yemen." Two schemes were proposed to deal with their pollution of the environment: making them of heavier plastic, which would keep them from taking flight, and breeding goats that could digest them. The plastic bag manufacturers easily blocked the former. No breed could be adapted to the latter.

14. Long hikes in Yemen's dramatic countryside were a favorite embassy activity, and scaling Noah's Ark was one of the more memorable such excursions.

15. The American Foundation for the Study of Man was a small institution led by Merilyn Phillips Hodgson, whose brother Wendell had been an "Indiana Jones" archaeologist excavating in Ma'rib in the 1950s. Wendell Phillips's account of that experience remains a great read.

16. "Remarks by the President on the Six-Month Anniversary."

17. President's Address to Congress on September 20, 2001.

18. Congressional Research Service (CRS) Report for Congress, "Middle East: U.S. Foreign Assistance, FY 2001, FY 2002 and FY 2003 Request," March 28, 2002. Ironically, as CRS noted, the expressed purpose of the FY 2002 supplemental was "to strengthen 'frontline states' in the war on terrorism."

19. In the FY 2003 request, the administration requested $5,264,200,000 for Israel, Egypt, Jordan, Lebanon, the West Bank/Gaza Strip, or related operations.

20. The United States objected to the Ottawa Convention on land mines to protect our use of them in Korea. Ironically, we then launched a significant practical

effort to help countries cope with the problem. In the late '90s, we were in a position to lead in funding Yemen's effort to remove mines, which had been laid primarily in the conflicts between North and South Yemen prior to unification in 1990. The Yemeni government publicized these efforts most effectively. The United States was always accorded pride of place for being the first significant international donor.

21. President Bush's Second Inaugural Address, January 20, 2005.

22. UN Development Program, *Arab Human Development Reports 2002–2009*, http://www.arab-hdr.org/. Presidential Adviser al-Iryani read drafts and advised the authors of this series of seminal reports.

23. Yemen's hydrocarbon resources are modest compared to its neighbors but very significant for its own economy. Yemen exported in 2004 oil worth $4.3 billion, which represented 70 percent of government revenue. See "Background Note: Yemen."

24. Abdulkarim had come up Hunt's ranks in Yemen and knew all aspects of its operations intimately. He was highly respected by his Yemeni counterparts. His wife, Lisa, had been a Peace Corps volunteer in Yemen—an Arabic speaker and a great asset.

25. The World Bank estimated that a Yemeni procurement of MiG-29 fighters from Russia would cost about $400 million, an enormous sum for impoverished Yemen. The Yemenis sought to justify the purchase as part of the war on terror, which was absurd since there was no reasonable scenario in which advanced fighters could be deployed against al Qaeda in Yemen. In 2008 the Center for Strategic and International Studies (CSIS) estimated there were eighteen MiG-29s in Yemen's inventory (see Anthony H. Cordesman, "Conventional Armed Forces in the Gulf: An Overview," June 23, 2008, http://csis.org/files/media/csis/pubs/080623_gulf milbal.pdf).

26. World Bank, "Yemen: Development Partners Affirm Support," October 17, 2002, http://web.worldbank.org/WBSITE/EXTERNAL/NEWS/0,,contentMDK:200 71483~menuPK:34466~pagePK:34370~piPK:34424~theSitePK:4607,00.html.

CHAPTER 6. INTO THE RED ZONE

1. We appreciated this measure all the more when one of Embassy Kuwait's walls was scaled by demonstrators, who succeeded in torching a number of embassy vehicles.

2. Questioning persuasively linked his motives to Palestine, with no link to al Qaeda.

3. In fact, in one instance, a Marine who had had trouble in a less demanding assignment was reassigned to Sanaa specifically because the commander believed the Marine detachment in Sanaa could sort out his problem. It did so.

4. Details were revealed in the course of the public trial of the plotters in 2004.

5. Of the six targets of this group, casing was most extensive against the American embassy, and weapons were procured and being modified for that attack.

6. The embassy had relatively sophisticated surveillance detection teams that occasionally reported suspicious activity, which was shared with Yemeni authorities. To my knowledge, neither we nor the Yemenis detected this casing.

7. *Terror in Yemen*, 20–23.

8. Indeed, protecting khat groves was a challenge. Stone towers from which owners could survey and aim at trespassers dotted the fields.

9. Many Arabs claim all terrorism in the Islamic world is spawned by the Palestinian question. Israelis and their supporters tend to deny any connection at all. In my experience, truth lies in between. Mujahideen see Palestine as one front among many—Afghanistan, Chechnya, Kashmir, the Gulf, and Yemen—in their jihad. Al Qaeda has sought to appropriate the popularity of the Palestinian cause while devoting few resources to it. Nevertheless, U.S.-Yemeni cooperation was significantly impeded in Yemen by negative developments in Palestine.

10. British prime minister Gordon Brown noted in a BBC interview on January 3, 2010, long-standing British-American cooperation in assisting Yemen in counterterrorism, http://news.bbc.co.uk/2/hi/8437757.stm.

11. *Yemen and the Confrontation with Terror*, selections from Speeches and Statements of President Ali Abdullah Saleh (in Arabic), Office of the President of the Republic, Army Information Center, March 2003, 119–120.

12. Almost invariably, terrorists leave clues behind in the debris of an attack. If the scene can be protected and then professionally processed, evidence related to the identities, linkages, and methods of the attackers can be gleaned.

13. However, Bill pointed out to me that much of the benefit to Jordan stemmed from trade privileges extended to the Jordanian-Israeli industrial zones. Rhetorically among the most anti-Israeli of Arabic countries, Yemen was very far indeed from matching Jordan's success in this regard.

14. After checking with Washington, I strongly discouraged Yemen's acceptance of

Iraqi largesse as a violation of UN sanctions. Of course, other Arab countries—Jordan and Syria in particular—did have similar arrangements to which the United States largely turned a blind eye. To my knowledge, the Yemenis never acted upon the Iraqi offer.

15. I had witnessed a similar phenomenon in Egypt during its successful campaign against the Egyptian Islamic Jihad and Gama'at al-Islamiyya in the mid-1990s. During a failed assassination attempt against an Egyptian official, terrorists killed a twelve-year-old Egyptian girl who became the symbol of Egyptian victims of terrorism. Subsequently, police pursuing terrorist assailants were pleasantly surprised to find that residents of the Cairo neighborhood into which the terrorists fled had captured and handed them over to authorities. At the time, the embassy noted the new phenomenon. A decade later, Egyptian prime minister Dr. Ahmed Nazif cited the incident in a presentation at the Council on Foreign Relations as a turning point in Egypt's campaign.

16. Proceedings of the trial in 2004.

17. *Terror in Yemen*, 26.

18. We had intelligence suggesting that the al Qaeda group believed the helicopter carried a VIP and speculated that the group believed I was aboard en route to Ma'rib. However, the trial records indicate that the helicopter itself and no specific individual were targeted.

19. The American Foundation for the Study of Man was engaged in excavating the Mahram Bilqis at the time and graciously briefed us on that project.

20. "The Government of Yemen has continued a broad counterterrorism campaign against al-Qaida and cooperated with the United States in eliminating Abu Ali al-Harithi, al-Qaida's senior leader in Yemen," *Patterns of Global Terrorism 2002*. As explained subsequently, this cooperation was and remains a subject of some sensitivity. For that reason, I am required to draw on public sources for much of what follows.

21. Walter Pincus, "U.S. Strike Kills Six in Al Qaeda," *Washington Post*, November 5, 2002.

22. James Bamford, "He's in the Backseat!" *The Atlantic*, April 2006.

23. "U.S. Missile Strike Kills al Qaeda Chief," CNN.com, November 5, 2002, http://archives.cnn.com/2002/WORLD/meast/11/05/yemen.blast/.

24. President George W. Bush, State of the Union address, January 28, 2003.

CHAPTER 7. THE SEASON OF ASSASSINATIONS

1. *Terror in Yemen*, 76–77.

2. Court records from the trial.

3. Rand subsequently resigned from the NSC staff because of disagreements on the direction of counterterrorism policy. He became a principal adviser on foreign affairs to Senator John Kerry's presidential campaign. In the Obama administration, he was appointed Department of Homeland Security under secretary for national protection and programs.

4. Brian Whitaker, "The 'So San' Affair," *Middle East International*, December 20, 2002. See also Glenn Kessler and Thomas E. Ricks, "U.S. Frees Ship with N. Korean Missiles; Stand Is Reversed after Yemen Protests Seizure of 15 Scuds," *Washington Post*, December 12, 2002.

5. White House press conference of Ari Fleischer, December 12, 2002.

6. Ibid.

7. The *So San* Affair was a factor leading to the Proliferation Security Initiative (PSI) announced by President Bush in Krakow, Poland, on May 31, 2003. The PSI was intended to fill legal gaps and create a community of nations working to halt proliferation of weapons of mass destruction and their delivery systems. Yemen did not join. For an analysis of international law and the *So San* Affair and its link to the PSI, see John Yoo and Glenn Sulmasy, "The Proliferation Security Initiative: A Model for International Cooperation," *Hofstra Law Review* 2, no. 35 (Winter 2006).

8. To my knowledge, the Yemenis fulfilled their commitment, and the missiles remained in their control. Yemen's arms relationship with North Korea was a matter of continuing interest to the United States since we had a policy to deny North Korea foreign exchange helpful in its nuclear or missile programs.

9. Conversely, President Bush took considerable political flak. See William Safire, "Bush's Stumble: The *So San* Affair," *New York Times*, December 19, 2002.

10. This directive resulted in the previously cited *Terror in Yemen*.

11. Patrick E. Tyler, "Yemen, an Uneasy Ally, Proves Adept at Playing Off Old Rivals," *New York Times*, December 19, 2002.

12. In early April 2002, *Al Mithaq*, the official newspaper of the ruling General People's Congress wrote, "Since he was appointed (last September), Ambassador Edmund Hull has behaved like a high commissioner, not like a diplomat in a

country which is opposed to any form of interference. . . . Edmund Hull adopts a very haughty behavior, far-removed from his diplomatic duties, when he speaks to certain Yemeni officials . . . [he is advised to] respect Yemen in order not to become persona non grata."

13. *Patterns of Global Terrorism 2002*, 64.

14. Mike Metrinko, the acting consul, led the embassy team, which included Vice Consul Randal Cunningham, regional medical officer Curt Hofer, and NCIS security officer Nick Butros. Their work won high praise from the Baptist Missions headquarters.

15. As part of our response, the embassy sent a magnetometer to the hospital so it could screen visitors for weapons. American personnel eventually returned and resumed their work with clear support from the local community. As a practical matter, they could not be secure. Despite a continuing threat, the Baptists reversed their decision to terminate their operation. Volunteers for duty in Jiblah multiplied. Hence, the terrorists produced exactly the opposite effect that they apparently intended. Kamal was tried, convicted, and, on November 27, 2005, executed.

16. The heretics included members of Yemen's historic Ismaili community, which number several thousand. Ali Jarallah was also tried, convicted, and, on November 27, 2005, executed. While some in the Yemeni Socialist Party suspected Islah or even government complicity, I know of no evidence that the assassinations were other than the act of an independent group led by Ali Jarallah.

17. Al-Moayad was convicted for providing material support to foreign terrorist organizations in New York in 2005 and sentenced to seventy-five years, but that conviction was overturned by the U.S. Court of Appeals in 2008 because the trial judge had allowed unrelated inflammatory material to influence the verdict. The matter was finally resolved in 2009 when al-Moayad pleaded guilty, was sentenced to time served, and soon deported back to Yemen. See John Marzulli, "Prominent Yemeni Cleric Mohamed Al-Moayad Pleads Guilty; Will Be Deported," NYDailyNews.com, August 7, 2009, http://www.nydailynews.com/news/national/2009/08/07/2009-08-07_prominent_yemeni_cleric_.html.

18. See "Two Die in Yemen after Anti-War Protest Turns Violent," PBS OnlineNews Hour, March 21, 2003, http://www.pbs.org/newshour/updates/protest_03-21-03.html.

19. U.S. embassies construct warden networks, involving key American contacts associated with business, schools, or other organizations, to facilitate communications and manage crises affecting the American community as a whole.

20. One targeted embassy employee moved into his office with his wife and their dog. With good spirits, they accepted the temporary inconvenience and then resumed their lives, albeit in a different residence, when all was clear. He was typical of Embassy Sanaa employees who served despite the general, and this personal threat.

21. *Mathbah* means slaughterhouse in Arabic.

CHAPTER 8. AN EMBASSY, NOT A BUNKER

1. In March 2002, terrorists threw grenades into an Islamabad church and killed five, including two Americans associated with the U.S. embassy. See *Patterns of Global Terrorism 2002*, 11.

2. State was not the only risk-adverse party. As noted above, the important Yemeni coast guard project remained moribund, despite a commitment by two combatant commanders to President Saleh, because lower levels in CENTCOM would not allow staffing of a coast guard adviser at the embassy.

3. Subsequently, in light of the demands of Iraq, Afghanistan, and elsewhere, USAID has created on Office of Transition Initiatives that addresses stabilization as a complement to its traditional development work.

4. Both groups have long been designated by the State Department as foreign terrorist organizations. See *Patterns of Global Terrorism 2002*.

5. During a visit to FBI headquarters in Washington, Foreign Minister al-Qirby commented in good humor about the relentless pressure I placed on the Yemenis for further cooperation on counterterrorism. Director Mueller expressed sympathy, noting that the ambassador was no less troublesome in pressing his own government, although admittedly in a good cause.

6. In his previous role as director general of the Foreign Service, Under Secretary Marc Grossman laid the groundwork for Powell's initiative.

CHAPTER 9. NOTHING IS AS GOOD AS IT SEEMS

1. Pakistan ($175 million) and Afghanistan ($170 million) also did well. Their funding, in my view, accurately reflected priorities in the war on terror. Jordan, while a staunch ally and an important front, received a disproportionate share.

2. Office of Management and Budget Passback Highlights on the president's FY 2003 budget for economic support funds.

3. The "zeroing out" of the military funds naturally elicited a protest from me. Unusually, this cry of pain elicited a response from the State Department, which agreed to re-program $5 million from another account. The commitment languished and might have been forgotten entirely but for timely reminders from the embassy. It was eventually transferred.

4. Indeed, numerous archaeological pieces were taken by American excavators under an agreement with the Yemeni government in the past and are part of the American Foundation for the Study of Man's collection in Northern Virginia. That practice had long been discontinued by the early 2000s.

5. In the 2001 parliamentary vote, more than fifty Yemenis died. In the 2003 vote, only three died. See NDI's report, "The April 27, 2003 Parliamentary Elections in The Republic of Yemen," April 27, 2003, http://www.accessdemocracy.org/files/1701_yem_elect-rep.pdf.

6. The sole European observer was an Italian socialist.

7. See NDI's statement, "Preliminary Statement of the NDI International Election Observer Delegation to Yemen's April 27 Legislative Elections," April 29, 2003, http://accessdemocracy.org/node/13169.

8. The Millennium Challenge was the signature development initiative of the George W. Bush administration. It sought to link economic assistance to reform. With countries that qualified with above-average scores on an array of political, economic, and social measures, the Millennium Challenge Corporations made compacts that included financing agreed projects with few bureaucratic restrictions.

9. Freedom House, "Global Freedom Gains amid Terror, Uncertainty: Surprising Level of Freedom in Poor Countries Found," press release, December 18, 2003, http://www.freedomhouse.org/template.cfm?page=70&release=62.

10. A German company was undertaking the actual demarcation of the agreed border.

11. The 1996 attack on Khobar Towers, in which nineteen U.S. Air Force personnel died, was perpetrated by Hezbollah with Iranian sponsorship, not al Qaeda.

12. President Bush's proclamation on Middle East democracy in his second inaugural amplified this effort and gave it a presidential stamp.

13. Article 98 of the treaty establishing the International Criminal Court provides for bilateral agreements between governments that preclude recourse to the court in dealing with relevant criminal cases.

14. Osama bin Laden, "A Message to the Iraqi People," Al Jazeera, October 18, 2003.
15. The iftar is the meal at sundown when Muslims break their fast during Ramadan. It is an occasion often used for honoring guests or friends.

CHAPTER 10. BACK ON TRACK

1. For the text, see http://www.al-bab.com/arab/docs/reform/sanaa2004.htm.
2. Yemen received an additional allotment of 86,700 metric tons of wheat.
3. Captain Innis's effort contrasted dramatically with a parallel one undertaken after the attack near Al Mukalla on the M/V *Limburg*. In a crash program financed by oil companies, patrol boats were procured to escort tankers. Since little or no provision was made for training or maintenance, Pakistanis had to be brought in to operate and maintain the craft. The program, despite ample funds, steadily deteriorated. Executives of the funding oil company eventually asked to meet with Bob and me in order to better understand the Yemeni Coast Guard success and to see if the mission of protecting the oil terminal at Ras Shihr could not be transferred to the Yemini Coast Guard.
4. An eighth, inoperable boat was supplied for spare parts. The Yemenis, at their own initiative and supported by Captain Innis, repaired it and brought it into operation.
5. U.S. Department of State, *Country Reports on Terrorism 2004*, 69.
6. Ibid.
7. Al-Nashari remains in U.S. custody as of this writing and presumably will face U.S. justice eventually. Al-Badawi's fate is addressed in the afterword.
8. The Sa'ilah was the watercourse through central Sanaa that flooded during the monsoon season. My predecessor had initiated funding of this project, which we maintained because it provided a great benefit to the residents of Sanaa and very high exposure for U.S. assistance. Our qamariya logos at major crossings were seen by tens of thousands of Yemenis as they made their daily commutes.
9. Born and raised in the Midwest corn and soybean belt, I had a firsthand acquaintance of America's agricultural prowess and also some feel for the political power of the farm vote, which safeguarded programs like 416b. My father, a frugal, non-farming man who raised eleven children, decried this government "giveaway" to his farming neighbors.
10. When we had attempted the visit a month previous, the governor had pleaded for delay. Although we were quite prepared to bring sleeping bags and camp the night, he insisted on a month's delay so he could accommodate us in style.

AFTERWORD

1. In January 2010, in the wake of the Christmas Day plot against Northwest Airlines flight 253, the Combating Terrorism Center at West Point published a special edition of its *CTC Sentinel* dedicated to the resurgence of al Qaeda terrorism in and from Yemen. According to Greg Johnsen, "Al-Qa'ida in Yemen was defeated by the close cooperation of the United States and Yemen during the first phase of the war (2000-2003), but it learned from the loss." See Johnsen, "Al-Qa'ida in Yemen's 2008 Campaign," *CTC Sentinel* 1, no. 5 (April 2008), republished in January 2010, 13. According to Brian O'Neill, "Al Qa'ida in Yemen had, before the destruction of its initial cadre around 2004, been largely as idiosyncratic in tactics and ideas as the country's politics." See O'Neill, "AQAP a Rising Threat in Yemen," *CTC Sentinel* 2, no. 4 (April 2009), republished in January 2010, 7–8.

2. On the outskirts of Sa'dah, Dar al-Hadith was founded by Muqbil al-Wadi'i, a Yemeni cleric trained in Saudi Arabia, in the late 1970s. See International Crisis Group, *Yemen: Defusing the Saada Time Bomb*, Crisis Group Middle East Report no. 86, May 27, 2009, 8–9, http://www.observatori.org/paises/pais_64/documentos/86_yemen___defusing_the_saada_time_bomb.pdf.

3. The Houthis were also vociferously anti-Israeli, but so was the Yemeni government.

4. Joost Hiltermann, "Disorder on the Border: Saudi Arabia's War inside Yemen," *Foreign Affairs,* December 16, 2009, http://www.foreignaffairs.com/articles/65730/joost-r-hiltermann/disorder-on-the-border. See also Jeremy M. Sharp, "Yemen: Background and U.S. Relations," *Congressional Research Service,* January 13, 2010.

5. For a detailed account of the Houthi rebellion, see International Crisis Group, *Yemen: Defusing the Saada Time Bomb.*

6. Such was the prevailing opinion at the Jamestown Foundation conference on Yemen, "Yemen on the Brink: Implications for U.S. Security Interests in the Horn of Africa," in Washington on April 15, 2010.

7. Steve Karam for years led the World Bank's port cities initiative. I knew his work well as he was an in-law through marriage to my wife's niece.

8. See Stephen Day, *The Political Challenge of Yemen's Southern Movement.* Carnegie Endowment for International Peace, Middle East Program, no. 108, March 2010.

9. Amb. Tom Krajeski, interview with author, April 13, 2010.

10. For Fadhli's calculus in switching allegiance, see Robert F. Worth, "Ex-Jihadist Defies Yemen's Leader, and Easy Labels," *New York Times,* February 26, 2010.

11. Krajeski, interview.

12. This explanation was given to the author by two experts close to the event: a diplomat and a senior official of a nongovernmental organization involved in the election. It is difficult for Americans long used to razor-thin victory margins to appreciate a Middle East psyche that would see a 77 percent positive vote as a defeat.

13. Threshhold status was a special category for countries that exhibited progress but needed help to qualify for regular Millennium Challenge status.

14. Ali Soufan, the FBI lead agent in the *Cole* case, remains an eloquent voice for justice in this regard. See Ali H. Soufan, "Coddling Terrorists in Yemen."

15. Given the extensive security cooperation between the two countries, I assume a suitable U.S. response could have been made in that domain with a more logical linkage to the offense.

16. Sharp, "Yemen," 28. It can be argued that ample international resources were available. Sharp also notes that in a London conference in November 2006, donors pledged $4.7 billion in assistance to Yemen for 2007–2010. However, only a small fraction of these pledges were realized because of donor concern about corruption. Also, these funds were not targeted, as the American program in 2001–4, on the deprived areas susceptible to becoming al Qaeda safe havens.

17. Dr. Ahmed Attieg, interview with author, April 16, 2010. Attieg was in charge of the embassy's health initiatives at this time.

18. Krajesky, interview.

19. David Finkel won a Pulitzer Prize for his three-part series in the *Washington Post* that detailed the problems of this undertaking: "Exporting Democracy: A Call from the Sheiks," December 18, 2005; "Exporting Democracy: A Place Called Al-Jawf," December 19, 2005; and "Exporting Democracy: The President's Concern," December 20, 2005.

20. The jailbreak was a virtual repeat of the breakout of the *Cole* suspects from a PSO jail in Aden on April 11, 2003.

21. Krajeski, interview.

22. This sketch of the jailbreak derives from accounts of American officials in Sanaa at the time and Andrew McGregor, "Yemen Convicts PSO Members Involved in February's Great Escape," *The Battle for Yemen,* 87.

23. Gregory D. Johnsen, "AQAP in Yemen and the Christmas Day Terrorist Attack," *CTC Sentinel,* January 2010, 2–3. The account of al Qaeda's resurgence in Yemen

is based primarily on the work of Greg Johnsen and secondarily on the work of Brian O'Ncill, which arc included the *CTC Sentinel*'s special January 2010 issue. Additional facts are provided by the Department of State's *Country Reports on Terrorism*.

24. U.S. Department of State, *Country Reports on Terrorism 2007 and 2008*.

25. U.S. Department of State, *Country Reports on Terrorism 2008: Middle East and North Africa Overview*, 16–17.

26. According to the State Department spokesman Sean McCormack, "the Embassy security upgrades that we have been putting in place over the past seven, eight years were, during this attack, effective in stopping the attack, along with the response of the Yemeni forces as well as the response of our American Embassy personnel." See U.S. Department of State, press briefing statement, September 17, 2008, http://montevideo.usembassy.gov/usaweb/2008/08-441EN.shtml.

27. U.S. Department of State, *Country Reports on Terrorism 2008*, 16.

28. Ibid.

29. Al Qaeda expert Bruce Riedel told a conference at the Jamestown Foundation on April 16, 2010, that Bin Nayyif would have been killed but for a last-minute slip by the assassin.

30. State Department coordinator for counterterrorism Daniel Benjamin in remarks at the Jamestown Foundation, April 16, 2010. As part of an assessment commissioned by Gen. David Petraeus upon taking charge of CENTCOM, his team flagged the situation in Yemen and provided a strategy paper. The author headed the counterterrorism team of that effort.

31. As noted in the introduction, the Central Command assessment team had recommended special attention and an approach to Yemen at the onset of General Petraeus's term.

32. Yemeni and American media also reported visits by CIA deputy director Stephen Kappes. For example, Lolita C. Baldor, "CIA Names New Deputy Director as Veteran Officer Steps Down," Associated Press, April 14, 2010.

33. The Yemeni National Security Bureau is roughly equivalent to the U.S. National Security Council.

34. Accounts of the incident are from Greg Johnsen, "The Expansion Strategy of Al-Qa'ida in the Arabian Peninsula," *CTC Sentinel* 2, no. 9 (September 2009), republished January 2010, 4. Johnsen's assessment of the impact of the AQAP

media strategy was confirmed to the author by an American journalist with extensive Yemeni experience.

35. Johnsen, "AQAP in Yemen."

36. Ibid.

37. Ibid.

38. Bill Roggio, "U.S. Launches Cruise Missiles against al Qaida in Yemen," *The Long War Journal*, December 19, 2009.

39. Such sums do not include additional funds from DoD and other agency accounts.

40. As I write this, I am mindful of recent reforms to decentralize responsibilities from ministries to governors in Yemen, but governors are appointed by the central government and, for my purposes, inherently extensions of it.

BIBLIOGRAPHY

"A Nation Challenged: Pursuing Al Qaeda; Yemen Adds Troops in Battle to Capture Suspects." *New York Times*, December 20, 2001.

Baldor, Lolita C. "CIA Names New Deputy as Veteran Officer Steps Down." Associated Press, April 14, 2010.

Bamford, James. "He's in the Backseat!" *The Atlantic*, April 2006.

Benjamin, Daniel, and Steven Simon. *The Next Attack: The Failure of the War on Terror and a Strategy for Getting It Right.* New York: Times Books, 2005.

bin Laden, Osama. "A Message to the Iraqi People." Al Jazeera, October 18, 2003.

Bowden, Mark. *Black Hawk Down: A Story of Modern War.* New York: Atlantic Monthly Press, 1999.

Brown, Gordon. Interview by Andrew Marr. *The Andrew Marr Show*, BBC One, January 3, 2010. http://news.bbc.co.uk/2/hi/8437757.stm.

Clarke, Richard A. *Against All Enemies: Inside America's War on Terror.* New York: Free Press, 2004.

Day, Stephen. *The Political Challenge of Yemen's Southern Movement.* Carnegie Endowment for International Peace, Middle East Program, no. 108 (March 2010).

Dresch, Paul. *Tribes, Government, and History in Yemen.* New York: Oxford University Press, 1989.

Feltman, Jeffrey D. *Yemen on the Brink: Implications for U.S. Policy.* Testimony for the House Committee on Foreign Affairs, Washington, February 3, 2010.

Finkel, David. "Exporting Democracy: A Call from the Sheiks." *Washington Post*, December 18, 2005:

————. "Exporting Democracy: A Place Called al-Jawf." *Washington Post*, December 19, 2005.

————. "Exporting Democracy: The President's Concern." *Washington Post*, December 20, 2005.

Freedom House. "Global Freedom Gains amid Terror, Uncertainty: Surprising Level of Freedom in Poor Countries Found." Press Release, December 18, 2003. http://www.freedomhouse.org/template.cfm?page=70&release=62.

Gettleman, Jeffrey. "Yemen, Once a Magnet, Now Expels Terrorists." *Los Angeles Times*, October 10, 2001.

Hiltermann, Joost. "Disorder on the Border: Saudi Arabia's War inside Yemen." *Foreign Affairs*, December 16, 2009. http://www.foreignaffairs.com/articles/65730/joost-r-hiltermann/disorder-on-the-border.

Human Rights Watch. *No Direction Home: Returns from Guantanamo to Yemen.* March 28, 2009.

International Crisis Group. *Yemen: Defusing the Saada Time Bomb.* Crisis Group Middle East Report no. 86, May 27, 2009. http://www.observatori.org/paises/pais_64/documentos/86_yemen___defusing_the_saada_time_bomb.pdf.

Johnsen, Gregory D. "Al Qa'ida in Yemen's 2008 Campaign." *CTC Sentinel* 1, no. 5 (April 2008). Republished in *CTC Sentinel*, special issue (January 2010).

Kessler, Glenn, and Thomas E. Ricks. "U.S. Frees Ship with N. Korean Missiles; Stand Is Reversed after Yemen Protests Seizure of 15 Scuds." *Washington Post*, December 12, 2002.

Kilcullen, David. *The Accidental Guerrilla: Fighting Small Wars in the Midst of a Big One.* New York: Oxford University Press, 2009.

Mackintosh-Smith, Tim. *Yemen: Travels in Dictionary Land.* London: John Murray, 1997.

Mardini, Ramzy. *The Battle for Yemen: Al Qaeda and the Struggle for Stability.* Washington: Jamestown Foundation, 2010.

Marzulli, John. "Prominent Yemeni Cleric Mohammed Al-Moayad Pleads Guilty; Will Be Deported." NYDailyNews.com, August 7, 2009.

McGregor, Andrew. "Yemen Convicts PSO Members Involved in February's Great Escape." *The Battle for Yemen*, Washington: Jamestown Foundation, 2010.

Naji, Abu Bakr. "The Management of Savagery: The Most Critical Stage through Which the Umma Will Pass." Translated by William McCants for the John M. Olin Institute for Strategic Studies at Harvard University, May 23, 2006.

National Commission on Terrorist Attacks upon the United States. *The 9/11 Commission Report: Final Report of the National Commission on Terrorist Attacks upon the United States.* New York: W. W. Norton, 2004.

O'Neill, Brian. "AQAP a Rising Threat in Yemen." *CTC Sentinel* 2, no. 4 (April 2009). Republished in *CTC Sentinel,* special issue (January 2010).

Pape, Robert A. *Dying to Win: The Strategic Logic of Suicide Terrorism.* New York: Random House, 2005.

Pincus, Walter. "U.S. Strike Kills Six in Al Qaeda." *Washington Post,* November 5, 2002.

Roggio, Bill. "U.S. Launches Cruise Missiles against al Qaida in Yemen." *The Long War Journal,* December 19, 2009.

Safire, William. "Bush's Stumble: The *So San* Affair." *New York Times,* December 19, 2002.

Sharp, Jeremy M. "Yemen: Background and U.S. Relations." *Congressional Research Service,* January 13, 2010.

Soufan, Ali H. "Coddling Terrorists in Yemen." *Washington Post,* May 17, 2008.

Soufan, Ali. Testimony to Senate Judiciary Committee, May 13, 2009. http://judiciary. senate.gov/hearings/testimony.cfm?id=3842&wit_id=7906.

Tenet, George. *At the Center of the Storm: My Years at the CIA.* New York: Harper-Collins, 2007.

Terror in Yemen: Where To? Sanaa, Yemen: 26th September Publications, December 2002.

Tyler, Patrick E. "In Washington, a Struggle to Define the Next Fight." *New York Times,* December 2, 2001.

———. "Yemen, an Uneasy Ally, Proves Adept at Playing Off Old Rivals." *New York Times,* December 19, 2002.

UN Development Program. *Arab Human Development Reports 2002–2009.* http:// www.arab-hdr.org//.

U.S. Department of State. *Country Reports on Terrorism.* 2004, 2005, 2006, 2007, 2008, 2009.

Whitaker, Brian. "The 'So San' Affair." *Middle East International,* December 20, 2002.

Worth, Robert F. "Ex-Jihadist Defies Yemen's Leader, and Easy Labels." *New York Times,* February 26, 2010.

"Yemen Confronting Terrorism: Selections from Speeches and Statements of President Ali Abdullah Saleh." Office of the President, March 2003.

Yoo, John, and Glenn Sulmasy. "The Proliferation Security Initiative: A Model for International Cooperation." *Hofstra Law Review* 2, no. 35 (Winter 2006).

INDEX

About the Author

In the aftermath of 9/11, Edmund J. Hull was sent as ambassador to the Republic of Yemen, where he served until mid-2004. Previously, he had served in both the Clinton and Bush administrations as deputy, then acting coordinator, for counterterrorism in the Department of State for which he received from the CIA the George H. W. Bush Award for Excellence in Counterterrorism. A career Foreign Service officer, he previously directed peacekeeping and humanitarian affairs in State's Bureau of International Organization and served at Embassy Cairo as both chargé d' affaires and deputy chief of mission. In the latter capacity, he was awarded the Baker-Wilkins Award for Excellence in the Direction and Management of Overseas Missions. His prior service also included director for Near East Affairs on the National Security Council. In this capacity he represented the NSC on the Baker Middle East shuttles, which culminated with the Madrid Conference. During Operation Desert Storm, he served as director for Northern Gulf Affairs (Iraq and Iran) in State. His overseas assignments also included political counselor at Embassy Tunis during the U.S.-PLO dialogue there, political-military officer at Embassy Cairo, and political officer at the Consulate General in Jerusalem during the Camp David process.

Ambassador Hull received his BA degree from Princeton University's Woodrow Wilson School of Public and International Affairs and was appointed its first diplomat-in-residence after departing Yemen. His courses there included Diplomacy, The Middle East Peace Process, Democratization in the Middle East, and National Intelligence. He also spent a year in mid-career at Oxford University studying under Sir Michael Howard. His first exposure to the Arab world came as a Peace Corps volunteer in

Tunisia from 1971 to 1973. Hull is married to Amal Abulhajj of Jerusalem, and they have two daughters, Leila and Lena. He currently consults with the U.S. military and was the team leader for counterterrorism in the Central Command Assessment done for Gen. David Petraeus upon his assumption of command. He lives in Washington, D.C., when not sailing aboard his thirty-four-foot Pacific Seacraft.